Developmentally Appropriate Middle Level Schools

2nd edition

M. Lee Manning
Old Dominion University

Association for Childhood Education International

www.acei.org • 17904 Georgia Ave., Ste. 215, Olney, MD 20832 • 800-423-3563

Anne W. Bauer, ACEI Editor
Bruce Herzig, ACEI Editor

Copyright © 2002, Association for Childhood Education International
17904 Georgia Ave., Ste. 215, Olney, MD 20832

Library of Congress Cataloging-in-Publication Data
Manning, M. Lee
   Developmentally appropriate middle level schools/M. Lee Manning.--2nd ed.
     p. cm.
  Includes bibliographic references (p.).
  ISBN 0-87173-156-8 (pbk.)
   1. Middle schools--United States. 2. Adolescence--United States. 3. Child
development--United States. I. Title.

LB1623.5 .M26 2002
373.236'0973--dc21

                  2002023606

Table of Contents

Preface

Researchers and writers have suggested that learners' developmental levels should provide the basis for school curricular and instructional practices, as well as the overall teaching-learning environment. While developmental psychologists offer insightful theories about physical, psychosocial, and cognitive development, the process of translating these theories into practice has been somewhat slow, especially beyond the elementary school years.

For decades, the role of schools for 10- to 15-year-olds remained unclear. The problem resulted from the mindset that elementary school should address education needs during the childhood years and secondary school should focus upon the adolescent years. Except for serving as a transition between elementary and secondary, the middle level school lacked a clear rationale. The growing middle level school movement represents a commitment to base school practices on 10- to 15-year-olds' unique developmental characteristics.

Several factors have contributed to an increased emphasis on developmentally responsive middle level schools. First, early adolescence has been accepted as a legitimate developmental period. Second, the middle level school has progressed beyond its infancy, developing to a stage where genuine improvements have been made. Third, the call for reforming middle level schools to be more responsive to young adolescents' needs has been widely disseminated through publications such as *This We Believe* (National Middle School Association, 1995), *Turning Points* (Carnegie Council on Adolescent Development, 1989), *Turning Points 2000* (Jackson & Davis, 2000), and the Association for Childhood Education International (ACEI) position paper on "Child-Centered Middle Schools" (ACEI/Manning, 2000). Fourth, educators' commitment to young adolescents' education and well-being has deepened, as evidenced by the continuing influence of ACEI's Intermediate/Middle Childhood Committee and the publication of the revised edition of this book.

Developmentally Appropriate Middle Level Schools examines early adolescence as a developmental period and explains the physical, psychosocial, and cognitive characteristics of 10- to 15-year-olds. In addition, it provides recommendations concerning how middle level schools can provide developmentally appropriate educational experiences.

Chapter 1 explores early adolescence as a developmental period, and its evolution toward acceptance. Contemporary efforts to promote the 10- to 15-year-old period are described. Chapter 2 examines contemporary research on physical, psychosocial, and cognitive development, and provides a developmental portrait of young adolescent learners. Chapter 3 shows how young adolescents' physical, psychosocial, and cognitive developmental characteristics can form the basis for developmentally appropriate curricular, instructional, and organizational decisions in middle level schools. Chapter 4 highlights resources for middle level school educators, including professional associations, Internet sites, and resource centers. Appendix A is a "Checklist To Determine Middle Level Schools' Response to Young Adolescents' Developmental Characteristics."

Advocates for effective middle level schools recognize the tremendous progress made during the last several decades, but they also realize that middle level schools are at a critical juncture. We have an improved understanding of 10- to 15-year-olds, we recognize the need for developmentally appropriate educational experiences, and we know the essentials of effective middle level schooling. Middle level educators must maintain the momentum, even in the midst of criticism. A forefather of the middle school movement, John Lounsbury (2000), noted there is "a charge to keep" (p. 193). There is indeed "a charge to keep" as we work toward improving young adolescents' education and well-being.

—**M. Lee Manning**

Chapter 1
Early Adolescence and Middle Level Schools

Questions To Be Explored

1. How did childhood, adolescence, and early adolescence become recognized as legitimate, distinct periods of growth and development?
2. What significant historical events mark the acceptance of early adolescence as a developmental period?
3. Which early researchers and writers contributed to the recognition of the 10- to 15-year-old age period as a legitimate developmental period?
4. What are middle level schools?
5. What is the preferred term for learners in this developmental period?
6. What challenges continue to hinder young adolescents and their education?
7. What are several models for developmentally appropriate middle level schools?
8. Why should and how can middle level educators work to re-engage parents and families in the education of young adolescents?

The acceptance of early adolescence as a distinct developmental period between childhood and adolescence and the emergence of the middle level school are relatively recent phenomena. Early adolescence (or the years 10 through 15) slowly gained recognition as a period of unique physical, psychosocial, and cognitive development. Despite criticism and skepticism, middle level schools are gaining acceptance as the most effective means of educating young adolescents. This chapter briefly examines the history of early adolescence as a developmental period, the history of the middle level school, and challenges for middle level educators wanting to provide developmentally appropriate school practices.

Young Adolescents and Middle Level Schools

To provide young adolescents with developmentally appropriate physical, psychosocial, and cognitive educational experiences, educators must have a clear understanding of terminology. Chart 1.1 looks at several crucial definitions.

Brief Historical Look at Childhood, Adolescence, and Early Adolescence

Chart 1.2 lists the important milestones in the acceptance of early adolescence as a unique developmental period.

Recognition of the Childhood and Adolescent Years

Childhood and adolescence had to be accepted as worthy and legitimate periods of development before early adolescence could be recognized. At one time, children were considered to be miniature adults with the cognitive and psychosocial capaci

Definitions

Young Adolescents
Students between the ages of 10-15 who experience the physical, psychosocial, and cognitive changes associated with the early adolescence developmental period, yet who also exhibit tremendous cultural, gender, developmental, and individual diversity that deserves to be considered by middle level school educators who plan educational experiences. (Manning & Bucher, 2001)

Developmentally Appropriate
Educational experiences that are appropriate for individuals' physical, psychosocial, and cognitive developmental needs and interests.

Child-Centered Middle School
The Association for Childhood Education International, and specifically the Intermediate/Middle Childhood Committee, defines the child-centered middle school as a school organization containing grades 6-8 (and sometimes grade 5) that provides 10- to 15-year-olds with developmentally appropriate and responsive curricular, instructional, organizational, guidance, and overall educational experiences in a safe, violence-free, and peaceful school; and that provides young adolescents with opportunities to participate in service learning, learn values, and develop citizenship and socialization skills. (ACEI/Manning, 2000)

Developmentally Appropriate Middle Level Schools
A school organizational approach, usually grades 6-8 and sometimes grade 5, that provides educational experiences designed specifically for young adolescents' physical, psychosocial, and cognitive developmental characteristics.

ties to act and think like adults. The young people who actually had access to schooling received a common set of experiences that did not recognize unique developmental needs and interests. The lack of knowledge about the childhood years contributed to children being treated alike and with little respect.

John Locke and Jean Jacques Rousseau made the first significant attempts to change prevailing attitudes toward children and the childhood years. Locke, in *Some Thoughts Concerning Education* (1693), stressed the uniqueness of the childhood years and the importance of recognizing children's development, needs, and interests. Similarly, Rousseau recognized children's developmental stages and agreed with Locke that childhood is a special time of life. In *Emile* (1762), Rousseau described children's growth and emphasized the necessity of learning experiences based on developmental levels.

Today's concept of adolescence might have originated with Rousseau's *Emile*

Chart 1.2
Selected Milestones:
Young Adolescents and Middle Level Schools

Date	Event	Implications
1904	G. Stanley Hall published two-volume work, *Adolescence*	First recognition of adolescence as a worthy period
1909	Junior high school (grades 7-9) established in Columbus, OH	First recognition that young adolescents need a school between the elementary and secondary schools
1918	National Education Association approves the junior high school	An educational association approves a school for this age group
1944	F. Redl published "Preadolescents: What Makes Them Tick?"	Preadolescence proposed as a developmental stage
1950	Middle school in Bay City, MI	First middle school established for young adolescents
1951	A. Blair and W. Burton published *Growth and Development of the Preadolescent*	An effort to study the psychology of preadolescence—a neglected field
1966	Donald Eichhorn published *The Middle School*	Proposed the importance of basing instruction on development
1968	R. Havighurst studied the middle school	Proposed that 10- to 14-year-olds experienced specific age-level developmental tasks
1972	J. Kagan and R. Coles published *Twelve to Sixteen: Early Adolescence*	Scholarly volume with 14 readings on 10- to 14-year-olds
1974	H. Thornburg published *Preadolescent Development*	Showed increasing acceptance of a specific developmental period for 10- to 14-year-olds
1977	J. Lipsitz published *Growing Up Forgotten*	Described the early adolescence developmental period as forgotten and needing attention
1981	H. Thornburg founded the *Journal of Early Adolescence*	The first scholarly research focusing on 10- to 14-year-olds
1983	G. Dorman published *Middle Grades Assessment Program* and "Making Schools Work for Young Adolescents"	Proposed that schools need to become more responsive to children's development
1984	J. Lipsitz published *Successful Schools for Young Adolescents*	Provided detailed descriptions of good middle level schools

Chart 1.2 (cont'd)
Selected Milestones:
Young Adolescents and Middle Level Schools

Date	Event	Implications
1989	Carnegie Council on Adolescent Development published *Turning Points*	Provided eight recommendations for transforming the education of young adolescents
1995	National Middle School Association published *This We Believe* (rev. ed.)	Position paper of the National Middle School Association
1997	*Phi Delta Kappa* published theme issue on "Middle Level Education and Reform"	Provided a look at impact of middle school reform efforts
2000	ACEI published "Child-Centered Middle Schools"	Position paper of the Association for Childhood Education International
2000	Anthony Jackson and Gayle Davis published *Turning Points 2000: Educating Adolescents in the 21st Century*	Carnegie Council's Report on progress since the 1989 *Turning Points*

(1762). In his attempt to clarify and extend the childhood stage, Rousseau characterized the period of adolescence as a second birth, or a time beyond the earlier period of childhood. In essence, "adolescence" was invented to provide for a time between childhood and adulthood, a time when a person is not a child yet does not have the authority to act, or the right to be treated, as an adult. Basically, society did not consider a person an adult until he or she could terminate schooling, work as an adult, or be convicted as a criminal. The concept of adolescence also resulted from a better understanding of human development. The first dramatic recognition of adolescence as a growth stage worthy of study can be found in G. Stanley Hall's two-volume work, *Adolescence*, published in 1904.

Recognition of Early Adolescence As a Legitimate Developmental Period Between Childhood and Adolescence

The legitimacy of early adolescence as a developmental period between childhood and adolescence has been accepted only during the past 30 or 40 years. Just as the childhood and adolescence stages received slow acceptance in some circles, legitimacy for the early adolescence developmental period was difficult to achieve. Between 1926 and 1974, fewer than 50 articles or books focused on the uniqueness of the age span (Thornburg, 1983). Havighurst (1968) gave credibility to early adolescence when he suggested developmental tasks for the age group, as did Thornburg (1983) when he described 10- to 15-year-olds' unique physical, psychosocial, and cognitive developmental characteristics.

As recognition of early adolescence increased, perceptive educators began calling attention to the need to base teaching-learning experiences on 10- to 15-year-olds' developmental characteristics. Eichhorn (1966) brought attention to the middle level school years and the importance of considering learners' development when planning and implementing instruction. Likewise, emphasis on the developmental period continued to increase as Havighurst (1968) recommended specific developmental tasks for middle level school children.

Increased use of the term "preadolescence" illustrated growing recognition of a developmental stage between childhood and adolescence. Then, "early adolescence" appeared to gain popularity, especially with the publication of *Twelve to Sixteen: Early Adolescence* (Kagan & Coles, 1972). In this text of collected readings, most of the authors referred to the developmental period as "early adolescence" and to individuals as "young adolescents."

During the early 1980s, Thornburg's contributions as a researcher and leader in the movement to understand early adolescence added to the credibility of the stage. In 1981, he founded the *Journal of Early Adolescence*, designed to provide a forum for researchers and writers interested in this unique developmental stage. After more than two decades, the journal continues to use the term "early adolescence" and to provide empirically based studies and theoretical articles on this developmental level. While the authors used terms interchangeably for a number of years (and in some cases still do), a major transition from "preadolescence" to "early adolescence" seemed to occur several years later.

While educators, developmentalists, and writers have accepted early adolescence as a legitimate developmental period, several questions continue to plague its advocates. First, what ages constitute this period? Should early adolescence include 9- to 14-year-olds, 9- to 15-year-olds, or 10- to 15-year-olds? Second, what one term should be used to designate these learners? They have been called "preadolescents," "emerging adolescents," "early adolescents," "in-between-agers," "transescents," and "young adolescents."

Growing Acceptance of the Early Adolescence Developmental Period, an Age Range, and a Designating Term

Books, journals, and other publications indicate a growing acceptance of the early adolescence developmental period, the age range of 10 to 15 years, and the designation "young adolescent." Also, nearly all state, corporation, and foundation reports use the term "young adolescent." A parallel may be drawn to the early childhood period and the designation "young children."

The National Middle School Association (NMSA) position paper, *This We Believe: Developmentally Responsive Middle Level Schools* (1995), refers to learners as "young adolescents." George and Alexander (1993) maintain that, regardless of the term used, "there is growing unanimity about the significance of this period of growing up" (p. 3).

To provide young adolescents with developmentally appropriate educational experiences, educators need to recognize early adolescence as a legitimate developmental period between childhood and adolescence. Just as educators no longer view children as miniature adults, they cannot perceive young adolescents as functioning in a land "somewhere in between" elementary and secondary school.

The Emergence of the Middle Level School

Neither children nor adults, young adolescent learners need effective school programs and practices that meet their unique developmental and educational needs. Young adolescents deserve schools that are more than a holding ground until they move on to secondary school. Developmentally appropriate middle level schools provide organizational and curricular responses designed to meet 10- to 15-year-olds' developmental needs while also acknowledging their tremendous diversity. Understanding the historical progression of the middle school can contribute to development of effective programs and practices.

Traditional School Organization

The eight-year elementary and four-year high school pattern dominated much of the 19th century. This 8-4 pattern provided large numbers of students with opportunities to learn basic skills and receive vocational training, and provided a smaller number with academic preparation for college. However, this organization did not adequately address the educational and developmental needs of young adolescents. Educators spent the next 100 years trying to develop a successful school in the middle (Manning, 2000).

Junior High Schools

At the turn of the century, school reform focused on the functions and relationships of the elementary school and the high school. The National Education Association (NEA) and other education groups advocated restructuring the predominant 8-4 organization to better serve the needs of young adolescents. In 1918, the NEA approved the junior high school concept. The first three-year junior high schools, incorporating grades 7-9, were established in Columbus, Ohio, in 1909. The junior high school had two overarching purposes: to enrich academic programs for college-bound students and to provide vocational programs for students expected to enter the job market in a few years (Manning, 2000).

Middle Level Schools

During the 1950s and 1960s, questions arose concerning whether the junior high school actually served the needs and interests of young adolescents. Debate over these concerns resulted in junior high school reform and the eventual emergence of the middle school. In 1950, the Bay City, Michigan, school system established the first middle school (Manning, 2000).

As research and scholarly writing provided more information on "what schools in the middle should be" and "what young adolescents are like," educators and proponents of middle schools reached an agreement that the middle school should be more than a copy of the elementary school. Its students differed from elementary students and deserved a school that addressed the unique needs of 10- to 15-year-olds, rather than those of 5- to 9-year-olds. A middle school effort emerged and essential middle school concepts developed. No longer was the middle school supposed to be an upward extension of the elementary school or an downward extension of the secondary school; it was now a school with its own mission: to address the unique physical, psychosocial, and cognitive developmental needs of 10- to 15-year-olds.

The middle school movement developed rapidly during the last several decades of the 20th century. The writings of such notable educators as Donald Eichhorn, William Alexander, John Lounsbury, Gordon Vars, Paul George, and Joan Lipsitz emphasized the characteristics of exemplary middle school practice. State reports, position papers, and textbooks provided specific directions for effective middle school practices. Middle level educators have a professional responsibility to consider these past perspectives, and to continue the push for effective middle schools that meet young adolescents' developmental needs.

Challenges to Middle Level Schools and Young Adolescents

Critics often take the middle school to task for its "child-centered" (Beane, 1999, p. 3) pedagogy, which they claim has failed with regard to academic achievement and behavior control (Beane, 1999; Saks, 1999). Lounsbury (2000), a powerful middle school advocate, addresses the following common criticisms of middle schools: its inclusiveness, the placement of cooperation over competition, and its lack of emphasis on a college preparatory curriculum. Beane (1999), another strong middle school advocate, considers middle schools to be "under siege" (p. 3). While "under siege" might be an exaggeration, some groups clearly disagree with the middle school concept as it moves beyond organizational matters toward full programmatic implementation (Lounsbury, 2000). Even in the face of such criticism, Dickinson (2001) argues that "there is nothing wrong with the middle school concept" (p. 1) and counters that, too often, "it is a phrase mindlessly uttered, but with no understanding of the real meaning or importance" (Dickinson, 2001, p. 4). Calling the middle school movement "the largest, most extensive educational reform of this century" (p. 193), Lounsbury (2000) challenges educators to support the tenets of the middle school movement and the effort to provide young adolescents with the schools they need and deserve.

Jackson and Davis (2000), in *Turning Points 2000,* maintain that middle level educators need more time to implement middle school concepts. Educators need to "dispel the belief that . . . gained some currency at the end of the 1990s that middle grades education has 'failed' " (p. 16). Developments over the last decade have taught educators that gains in academic achievement and other positive outcomes for students require comprehensive implementation of reforms over an extended period of time (Jackson & Davis, 2000). Some observers have suggested that middle school educators misinterpreted the recommendations of *Turning Points* (Carnegie Council on Adolescent Development, 1989), emphasizing social and emotional development and equity over academic achievement (Elmore, 2000).

As the movement to reform middle level schools gains momentum, the following challenges remain:

- Knowledge about the early adolescence period, and the dramatic and rapid biological, social, emotional, and cognitive changes that characterize it, continues to be somewhat limited, especially compared to other developmental stages.
- Instead of developmentally appropriate education, young adolescents often receive curricular and instructional experiences that are either a repeat of elementary school experiences or a "watered-down version" of secondary school experiences.
- Young adolescents continue to be viewed by some educators and lay people as developmentally "somewhere between" childhood and adolescence, simply "too old to be children yet too young to be adolescents."
- Young adolescents sometimes have a reputation for being a rowdy and misbehaving group, difficult to teach and manage.
- Young adolescents often attend middle level schools that continue to subscribe to the "transitional schools" role—schools that merely house learners between elementary and secondary school.
- Young adolescents often attend schools staffed by teachers and administrators who have been trained and certified to work in either elementary or secondary schools and who consequently know little about young adolescents and their development.
- Young adolescents often attend middle level schools that place major emphasis (or the only emphasis) on school organization. These schools fail to develop a genuine middle level curriculum or an educational environment conducive to academic, personal, and social growth.
- Young adolescents are too often considered a homogeneous group, without regard for their gender, cultural, social class, and individual differences.

Promising Directions for Schooling Young Adolescents

Even considering the critics, there are promising signs for middle schools. The Association for Childhood Education International and its Intermediate/Middle Childhood Committee, the National Middle School Association and its state affiliates, the National Association of Secondary School Principals, and various other associations are calling for effective middle school education and providing direction for its implementation. The number of researchers, authors, and scholars in this field continues to grow. The research base on both middle school education and young adolescents has increased steadily in both quantity and quality. Several textbooks now identify what educators need to know to become effective teachers of young adolescents. The future of middle schools looks positive. We know what should be done and the momentum continues; the movement looks strong, thanks to the many educators who work in middle schools on a daily basis. The middle school has grown beyond its infancy stage and is weathering the criticisms. It is a school unique to itself and has "come of age" (Manning & Bucher, 2001, p. 286).

Several additional indicators suggest a growing interest in the early adolescence developmental period and the need for effective middle level school practices: 1) journal efforts such as *Phi Delta Kappan's* issue on Middle Level Education and Reform (March 1997); 2) the release of several middle level school textbooks, including *Teaching in the Middle School* (Manning & Bucher, 2001) and *Teaching Ten to Fourteen Year Olds* (Stevenson, 1998); and 3) efforts by ACEI and its Intermediate/Middle Childhood Committee to improve the lives and educational experiences of young adolescents (e.g., the publication of its position paper on "Child-Centered Middle Schools" [ACEI/Manning, 2000]). These efforts suggest important contemporary directions for the middle school movement, such as:

- Providing a curriculum that has a middle level school identity distinctly reflecting 10- to 15-year-olds' developmental characteristics
- Providing curricular, organizational, and instructional practices that reflect young adolescents' development
- Understanding developmental, cultural, gender, and socioeconomic differences among young adolescents
- Taking advantage of the national emphasis (represented by reports, documents, and articles) on the early adolescence developmental period
- Understanding the relationships between young adolescents and their families.

Middle level educators share a commitment to provide 10- to 15-year-olds with developmentally appropriate educational experiences. Efforts in this direction include:

- Promoting the general welfare of young adolescents through personal contact with parents, parent-teacher conferences, advisory councils, school boards, social service agencies, and community organizations
- Learning more about the lives of young adolescents, including friendships, peer pressure, parent and family relationships, cognitive levels, and socialization
- Insisting on continued recognition and acceptance of the early adolescence developmental period and the necessity of educational experiences that reflect neither elementary nor secondary orientations
- Insisting that administrators, teachers, counselors, and other middle level school personnel be professionally trained to work with young adolescents.

Historical observations show a rocky road from the early perception of children as miniature adults to the present acceptance of early adolescence as 10- to 15-year-olds' unique developmental period. Advocates for improving the lives and educational experiences of young adolescents can take pride in recent accomplishments. Challenges undoubtedly will remain as administrators and teachers work toward improving educational opportunities for young adolescents.

Models for Developmentally Appropriate Middle Level Schools

The most effective middle level schools readily demonstrate a willingness and ability to base school experiences on young adolescents' physical, psychosocial, and cognitive developmental characteristics. In essence, the common theme is that middle level schools should emphasize academic excellence *and* (italics Elmore's) provide developmentally appropriate, equitable education (Elmore, 2000).

Middle level school educators can use the developmental characteristics outlined in Chapter 2 and several models as they implement developmentally appropriate and child-centered middle schools. While other models undoubtedly exist, the three shown here have solid potential for middle level schools. They include *This We Believe: Developmentally Responsive Middle Level Schools* (National Middle School Association, 1995), *Turning Points* (Carnegie Council on Adolescent Development, 1989), and ACEI's "Child-Centered Middle Schools: A Position Paper" (ACEI/Manning, 2000). Middle level school educators could adopt either of these models as a basis for their school or choose those elements from the models that they deem most appropriate for their particular middle school.

This We Believe (National Middle School Association, 1995), a consensus statement on middle level school education, defines the middle level school as "the seg-

---

Chart 1.3
NMSA's Position Paper on Developmentally Responsive Middle Level Schools

Developmentally Responsive Middle Level Schools Are Characterized by:
- Educators committed to young adolescents
- A shared vision
- High expectations for all
- An adult advocate for every student
- Family and community partnerships
- A positive school climate.

Therefore, Developmentally Responsive Middle Level Schools Provide:
- Curriculum that is challenging, integrative, and exploratory
- Varied teaching and learning approaches
- Assessment and evaluation that promote learning
- Flexible organizational structures
- Programs and policies that foster health, wellness, and safety
- Comprehensive guidance and support services.

Source: National Middle School Association. (1995). *This we believe: Developmentally responsive middle level schools.* Columbus, OH: Author. Reprinted by permission.

---

ment of schooling that encompasses early adolescence, the stage of life between the ages of 10 and 15. In order to be developmentally responsive, middle level schools must be grounded in the diverse characteristics and needs of these young people" (p. 5). A true middle level school has 10 essential elements: educators who are knowledgeable about 10- to 15-year-olds, a balanced curriculum based on developmental needs, a range of organizational strategies, varied instructional strategies, an exploratory program, comprehensive advisory and counseling programs, continuous progress, appropriate evaluation procedures, cooperative planning, and a positive school climate. Chart 1.3 summarizes the positions and perspectives of *This We Believe*: *Developmentally Responsive Middle Level Schools*.

Turning Points (Carnegie Council on Adolescent Development, 1989) contains recommendations for improving the educational experiences of all middle level students, including those at risk of being left behind. Chart 1.4 summarizes the recommendations and appropriate practices described in *Turning Points*.

ACEI and its Intermediate/Middle Childhood Committee prepared a position paper on child-centered middle schools. Chart 1.5 summarizes this document's recommendations for developmentally appropriate practice.

Re-engaging Parents: Essential to All Middle Level School Efforts

Parents' participation in the life of the school and in their children's schoolwork has a positive impact on student outcomes (Jackson & Davis, 2000), yet some parents seem to need more guidance from educators when their children reach the middle grades. Changes in school practice, in family status, and in the larger society all contribute to the declining involvement of parents at the middle level (Brough & Irvin, 2001). The specific reasons for limited school contact by parents of middle school students vary. Parents of young adolescents often misinterpret their children's push for greater independence as a signal to disengage from their schools (Downs, 2001). Middle grades educators bear the responsibility to determine reasons for parental non-involvement (Brough & Irvin, 2001) and counter them.

One parent of a young adolescent admitted that she played a small role in her 7th-grade daughter's education. She said, "Well, first, Jill does not want me at school and, also, I think her teachers are doing an alright job. Jill is not in elementary school anymore, and she really does not need me there." The guidance counselor tried to explain the need for her to take a greater role in her daughter's education. She explained that even 7th-graders, and their teachers, benefit from having parents involved in education.

Effective middle level educators work closely with parents and the communities. Volunteers and guests enrich the instructional program and provide important benefits for both school and community. Also, cooperative involvement and relationships enhance the quality of instruction and learning in middle level schools. The best schools encourage parental support in addressing young adolescents' physical, social, and cognitive development and their striving toward independence. In many communities, however, parents still do not play integral roles in middle level schools.

Chart 1.4
Recommendations and Appropriate Practices
From *Turning Points*

Recommendations	Appropriate Practices
1. Create small communities for learning	Opportunities for intellectual and personal growth where stable, close, and mutual respectful relationships exist: schools-within-schools, teams, and small group advisories
2. Teach an academic core	Opportunities to build literacy, develop thinking skills, lead a healthy life, behave ethically, and assume responsibility in a pluralistic society
3. Ensure success for all students	Opportunities for all students to experience success—elimination of tracking by achievement level, promotion of cooperative learning, flexibility in instructional time, and adequate resources
4. Empower teachers and administrators to make decisions regarding educational experiences	Opportunities for students to have teachers with greater control over decisions affecting the education process
5. Staff middle schools with teachers who are expert at teaching 10- to 14-year-olds	Opportunities for students to have teachers who are properly prepared and assigned
6. Improve academic performances by fostering health and fitness	Opportunities for students to have access to health coordinators and to health care and counseling services, and access to a health-promoting school environment
7. Re-engage families in the education of learners	Opportunities for parents to act in meaningful roles in school governance, opportunities to support the learning process at both home and school
8. Connect schools with communities	Opportunities for student participation in the community through service and partnerships

Adapted with permission from Carnegie Council on Adolescent Development. (1989). *Turning points: Preparing American youth for the 21st century.* Washington, DC: Author. This report was prepared by the Carnegie Council on Adolescent Development's Task Force on Education of Young Adolescents. The Carnegie Council is a program of Carnegie Corporations of New York.

Re-engaging Parents and Families: A Rationale

The need to re-engage parents and families in the education of their young adolescents has never been clearer. Partnerships between parents and school personnel enhance the education of young adolescents. They also provide parents with opportunities to play crucial roles in ensuring their children's health and safety, in preparing them for school, and in creating a home environment that contributes to school achievement and overall development. When parents become knowledgeable partners with schools concerning their children's education, students' schoolwork, attitudes, and aspirations for continued schooling all improve. Instead of only calling parents when their children are in trouble or asking them to perform peripheral tasks far removed from instruction, effective programs adopt a more inclusive approach that welcomes parents as full partners in the education process (Downs, 2001).

Suggestions for Re-engaging Parents and Families

Through memos, notices, report cards, and conferences, educators can recommend ways parents can assist young adolescents at home. They can invite parents to

---

Chart 1.5
ACEI's Recommendations for Child-Centered Middle Schools

ACEI and its Intermediate/Middle Childhood Committe have taken a strong stance to promote child-centered middle schools that:

- Base educational experiences on young adolescents' physical, psychosocial, and cognitive development
- Provide teachers who are trained in middle school concepts and early adolescence development
- Provide exploratory programs, both curricular and special interest
- Provide interdisciplinary teaming
- Provide comprehensive guidance and counseling programs
- Provide flexible scheduling and variable learning group sizes
- Ensure equal access to all educational experiences
- Harbor high expectations for all young adolescents, both for behavior and academics
- Ensure a positive and safe learning environment
- Advocate service learning as an essential aspect of the curriculum
- Offer curricular experiences that are integrative, exploratory, and developmentally appropriate
- Involve immediate and extended family as well as community members.

Developed from: ACEI/Manning, M. L. (2000). Child-centered middle schools: A position paper. *Childhood Education, 76*(3), 154-159.

---

attend student performances and participate in classroom activities. Finally, parents can be encouraged to join advisory councils and advocacy groups at the school, district, or state level that monitor schools and work for school improvement. Parent-teacher organizations represent another important way in which schools can reach out to involve parents. These organizations can be particularly important in offering parents opportunities to decide what they need to know about early adolescence. Participation on school-wide building governance committees also provides parents with meaningful opportunities to help define the school's mission and to join in decision-making. The parents' role must be carefully defined to complement rather than conflict with the school staff's role in developing the academic program (Jackson & Davis, 2000).

Efforts to re-engage parents and schools encourage parents to take several initiatives, including: 1) talking to children about schoolwork and becoming actively involved in their school life, 2) setting and enforcing rules on homework and television watching, and 3) ensuring that children get to school on time. Likewise, schools and communities can provide more involvement opportunities for parents and, in some cases, create programs that help parents guide children through school. Other school efforts include meeting with individual parents, sending notes home about children's performance, and holding school meetings at times convenient for working parents.

Schools can promote trust, collaboration, and communication between parents and schools by:

- Assigning each student an adviser for the entire period of enrollment, who comes to know the student's family personally
- Forging alliances with parents in planning a course of study during the middle grade years that will enable children to reach their full potential
- Encouraging parents to participate with their child in conferences with teachers
- Encouraging parents to tutor young adolescents or monitor their completion of homework
- Designing home-learning activities that draw on parents' strengths. (Jackson & Davis, 2000)

The strongest correlation to school achievement comes from home-based activities. For example, 8th-graders who reported having home discussions about their studies almost every day had the highest average reading scores in the 1999 National Assessment of Educational Progress (Downs, 2001).

Effective parental programs and efforts include:

- Sunset Middle School (Longmont, Colorado) has specifically designed programs to involve parents. They supervise a reception area for students and their parents; recruit and train mentors for troubled students and their parents; and perform a wide range of volunteer activities, including raising money for school activities and assisting teachers in their classrooms.

- Rogers Middle School (Long Beach, California) actively engages parents in reforms tied to academic standards. The school provides parents with daily agenda planners printed with the rubrics for individual assignments, as well as a school rubric that details the qualities of good writing.
- Parents at Conway Middle School (Louisville, Kentucky) have been instrumental in helping students switch to student-led conferences, in which students are more responsible for their learning and for reporting their school progress.
- At Gunston Middle School (Arlington, Virginia), parents can check out student-created videos from the school library. The videos show parents how to help their children develop good science projects, how to get them involved in after-school tasks, and other valuable topics (Downs, 2001).
- Kernersville Middle School (Winston-Salem, North Carolina) and Meadowlark Middle School (Lewisville, North Carolina) have adopted the Victory in Partnership (VIP) program, which ensures that parents will receive weekly academic updates about their children (L'Esperance & Gabbard, 2001).
- Jamestown Middle School (Jamestown, North Carolina) has substantially increased the representation of minority parents on school committees by inviting them to a series of workshops and seeking advice about school improvement plans (L'Esperance & Gabbard, 2001).

Downs (2001) identifies six key areas for effective parent efforts: communicating with parents about school programs and student progress, assisting parents with parenting skills, stressing the importance of volunteering, including parents in decision-making, showing parents how to expand learning activities at home, and collaborating with the community to coordinate resources and services for families.

Concluding Remarks

During the past several decades, serious efforts have been made to understand young adolescents and to implement middle level school practices that reflect their physical, psychosocial, and cognitive development. Respected publications have called for increased attention to 10- to 15-year-olds, and for reform of middle level school practices. The momentum must not be lost. Lounsbury's (2000) statement is worth repeating—middle level educators have "a charge to keep" (p. 193). Educators have the professional responsibility to act as advocates for young adolescents and to insist on effective middle level schools that meet young adolescents' developmental needs.

Chapter 2
Physical, Psychosocial, and Cognitive Development

Questions To Be Explored

1. What changes, constants, and concerns do young adolescents experience?
2. What physical, psychosocial, and cognitive characteristics identify learners in the early adolescence developmental period?
3. How does the considerable diversity in developmental rates during early adolescence affect teaching-learning experiences?
4. What are the implications of young adolescents' physical, psychosocial, and cognitive development for designing and implementing developmentally appropriate curricular and instructional practices?
5. What gender and cultural differences warrant understanding and consideration in planning developmentally appropriate middle level schools?
6. What educational practices, environmental conditions, and school policies can educators assess to determine whether a middle level school provides developmentally appropriate experiences?

Dramatic physical, psychosocial, and cognitive changes occur daily during early adolescence. These have significant implications—both for the 10- to 15-year-olds experiencing the changes and for educators planning developmentally appropriate middle level schools to serve them. Young adolescents have concerns about the normalcy of their development, while middle level school educators are responsible for basing curricular and instructional practices on young adolescents' development. Emphasizing the need to understand their development, this chapter examines the physical, psychosocial, and cognitive characteristics of 10- to 15-year-olds and reviews the implications for middle level educators.

The Need To Understand and Respond to Young Adolescents' Development

An understanding of young adolescents reveals tremendous diversity among their development, maturity levels, behavior, and sometimes rapidly fluctuating self-esteem. Such understanding provides insight into young adolescents' concerns and questions about overall development, body changes, and the onset of puberty.

Equally important is the educator's commitment to provide these students with developmentally appropriate teaching. Effective middle level educators play a significant role in helping learners understand the developmental changes affecting them, the nature of changing friendships and peer relations, and their shifting allegiance from family to peers.

One middle level school included young adolescent development as a major topic in its advisory program. The educators carefully selected topics for each of the three grade levels. For example, friendship formation was addressed in the 6th grade, peer pressure in the 7th grade, and handling disputes and sustaining long-term friendships in the 8th grade. The carefully sequenced program taught young adolescents about their development and the normalcy of developmental diversity.

Educational practices should demonstrate that developmentally appropriate instruction has been planned and implemented. Physical development may require that young adolescents have frequent opportunities to stretch or exercise, psychosocial development may affect peer and friend relationships, and cognitive development may contribute to higher levels of thinking and less egocentrism. Developmentally appropriate educational experiences include opportunities for young adolescents to behave responsibly and practice self-discipline; develop physical skills; explore aptitudes, interests, and special talents; and develop positive self-esteem. In essence, young adolescents benefit, both as individuals and learners, when educational experiences reflect developmental characteristics and changes.

Young Adolescents: Changes, Constants, and Concerns

Young adolescents experience numerous changes, constants, and concerns during this rapid developmental period. Chart 2.1 provides a glimpse into many young adolescents' lives.

These changes, constants, and concerns have a profound effect on young adolescents. A young adolescent's feelings of clumsiness or awkwardness might lead to feelings of worthlessness or isolation. Likewise, being unable to succeed at higher-level problem-solving activities when others can may lead to feelings of inferiority or lower self-esteem. One physically small 7th-grade boy, the victim of bullies, doubted his ability to cope with the school day. He was harassed on his way to and from school, and while at school. A constant bombardment of verbal and physical threats took a serious toll on his self-esteem. Fortunately, one middle school teacher understood how physical size can affect self-esteem, and worked to help the young boy develop a better perception of himself and his abilities. Realizing that all developmental changes can lead to behavioral changes, caring educators remember that young adolescents need security and acceptance, even when the students' behaviors and attitudes challenge their understanding and patience.

Young Adolescents' Development: Interconnected and Diverse

Perceptive middle level educators understand that young adolescents' physical, psychosocial, and cognitive development is interconnected, with one developmental area affecting another. A common mistake is to speak of young adolescents' physical, psychosocial, and cognitive development as if each type occurred in isolation; in fact, the developmental areas interrelate. For example, the young adolescent preoccupied with early or late physical development may delay social interaction or cognitive endeavors until reaching a satisfactory resolution concerning physical development. While this book examines physical, psychosocial, and cognitive areas

Chart 2.1
Changes, Constants, and Concerns

Changes

Young adolescents experience:
- Changing physical development and appearances
- Expanding social worlds
- Shifting allegiance from parents to peers
- Advancing cognitive capabilities.

Constants

Young adolescents need:
- Acceptance from peers, families, and educators
- Physically and psychologically safe and secure learning environments
- Love and acceptance, regardless of developmental changes and appearances
- Optimistic perspectives on life that provide a sense of stability and security.

Concerns

Young adolescents experience:
- Concerns about developmental changes and individual differences in development rates
- Changes in friendships and family relationships
- Peer pressure to dress and behave in a certain way
- Lower self-esteem, often without an understanding of why they feel that way.

separately for reasons of clarity, readers should remember the continuous and interconnected nature of development at all levels.

It is also essential for middle level educators to recognize the tremendous diversity among and within young adolescents, and recognize how this diversity affects the interconnectedness of overall development. It is difficult to describe the "young adolescent" boy or girl. Young adolescents differ in physical, psychosocial, and cognitive development; gender; ethnicity and culture; social class; and sexual orientation. Referring to a boy or girl as a 13-year-old or a 14-year-old communicates little except chronological age. Two 13-year-olds can differ in many ways (e.g., size, physical appearance, social maturity, and cognitive reasoning). Middle level educators need to consider overall development, individual differences, and varying developmental rates when making curricular, organizational, instructional, and managerial decisions.

One student teacher explained, "I saw a 15-year-old boy. He was physically mature, well-developed, and probably about as physically big as he would grow to be. Upon a closer observation, I realized he was far less developed psychosocially and cognitively. He was painfully shy and immature. Cognitively, at least in some areas, he was still functioning in the concrete operations stage. That taught me I should not make assumptions based on physical appearances."

Physical Development

Physical Characteristics of Young Adolescents

Physical development can be defined as the growth and development of the physique or the skeletal, structural, and muscular system (Manning & Bucher, 2001). One can identify several physical developmental characteristics that contribute to a portrait of young adolescents and allow credible generalizations. It remains important to remember, however, that individual development varies according to genetics, culture, gender, and socioeconomic status.

Characteristic 1. Young adolescents experience a growth spurt marked by a rapid increase in body size, as well as readily apparent skeletal and structural changes.

The first outward sign of puberty is the rapid gain in height and weight known as the growth spurt (Berk, 2001, p. 352). Rapid and profound growth spurts and other closely related physical developmental changes are easily recognized in both boys and girls (Papalia, Olds, & Feldman, 2001). While diversity in development must be remembered, the growth spurt normally occurs between ages 10 and 15. Common changes include growth in body size and the development of the primary and secondary sex characteristics.

J. M. Tanner (1973) conducted the classic studies on "growing up" that continue to provide the basis for much of today's writings on young adolescents' physical development. He concluded that growth spurts differ for boys and girls and that, on the average, the growth spurt comes two years earlier in girls than in boys. The average boy is slightly taller than the average girl until the girl's growth spurt begins. At about the age of 11 to 13, the average girl may grow taller and may be heavier and stronger (Tanner, 1973).

Both boys and girls grow at faster rates than they have ever experienced, with the exception of the infancy years. During the approximately two years of the growth spurt, 9 to 10 inches of growth for boys and 7 inches for girls sometimes occur. For a time, girls weigh more than boys (Milgram, 1992).

Some body parts grow faster than others. For example, legs most often reach their growth peak first; then, the trunk follows. The sequence of growth and the temporary mismatch of body parts often make 10- to 15-year-olds feel ungainly, awkward, and uncoordinated. Both girls and boys develop a preoccupation with their changing bodies and constantly examine their physical appearance for signs of imperfections. One 12-year-old once said, "I hope my parents and friends will like me no matter how I look when I am grown up." During this young girl's rapid development, she needed love, acceptance, and a sense of safety and security. Likewise, her teachers needed to provide a nonthreatening classroom environment that nurtured her delicate and changing self-esteem.

Today's young adolescents are bigger than in previous generations. The average girl today is 1/2 to 1 inch taller than her mother and reaches menarche (a female's first menstrual period) nearly a year sooner. In the late 1800s, boys did not reach their full height until at least age 23; now, most boys reach adult height by age 18 (Milgram, 1992). This earlier maturation is the result of several factors, including nutrition and quality of medical care.

Several readily apparent structural and skeletal changes serve as indicators of maturing individuals. Substantial changes in limb length, hip width, and chest breadth and depth often occur rapidly. A more adult look develops. Boys' voices deepen, their shoulders grow wider, and pubic and facial hair becomes visible. Similarly, girls' hips widen and pubic hair appears. Physical changes interrelate with cognitive, social, and emotional development; the advent of a physically developed body does not imply maturity in other developmental areas.

Characteristic 2. *Young adolescents experience the same developmental sequence, but rates and growth spurts vary among individuals.*

As long as developmental issues have been studied, the sequence of developmental changes has remained constant. In general, girls develop two years ahead of boys, but considerable variability exists in terms of when the development begins. The ages of greatest variability in the maturation of girls are 11, 12, and 13; for boys, the greatest variations occur during ages 13 and 14. Similarly, differences in developmental rates vary among same-sex young adolescents. One boy may have completed a growth cycle, while another boy of the same age may not even have started the growth cycle. Another 14-year-old boy may be developing at such a rapid pace that he resembles a 17-year-old, while another boy of the same age resembles a 12-year-old. One 12-year-old girl might be an early maturer who is preoccupied with self and friends and demonstrates higher levels of thought, while another might be just starting to grow or develop into puberty, be very dependent upon her parents and a few close friends, and think only in concrete terms. Rates of development have the potential for weighing heavily on young adolescents and can affect other areas such as self-esteem and general psychosocial development.

In one 7th-grade mathematics class, most of the boys were physically large; however, one boy looked like he should have been in about the 3rd or 4th grade. It was a textbook example of physical diversity in middle level schools. Five boys, including the smaller boy, were working in a collaborative group. The observer asked the teacher how well the larger boys worked with the smaller boy. The teacher explained that the smaller boy was fortunate, as the larger boys felt a degree of responsibility for his well-being.

Characteristic 3. *With the onset of puberty, young adolescents experience physiological changes that include development of the reproductive system.*

Closely associated with these growth spurts and changes in height and weight is the onset of puberty, often considered the most intense and rapid of any developmental stage. The gross motor performance that accompanies puberty differs for girls and boys. Girls' gains are often slow and gradual, leveling off by age 14. In contrast, boys show a dramatic spurt in strength and endurance that continues through the teenage years (Berk, 2001).

The onset of puberty is difficult to assess in males and is usually based on the development of secondary sex characteristics and the growth of the genitalia. In females, the first menstrual period is usually considered to be the onset of puberty. While a wide age range for pubertal changes exist, most girls and boys reach puberty during the middle level school years.

Whatever indicators of puberty educators choose to recognize, the development of the reproductive system during this stage makes reproduction possible. Female hormones develop between the ages of 9 and 12 and mark the beginning of a long series of psychological and physical changes that transform girls into women. In the case of boys, the increase in male hormones is less accentuated and occurs over a greater period of time. Both girls and boys begin to develop a sexual identity (Papalia, Olds, & Feldman, 2001).

Although young adolescents' tremendous diversity makes age-developmental norms difficult to determine, teachers can expect these students to experience significant and possibly discomforting pubertal changes and rapid growth spurts. Middle level educators sometimes find young adolescents to be preoccupied with these changes. Such preoccupation can affect their attention, motivation, and capacity to focus on school learning activities. Puberty also can result in increased child-parent conflicts, as young adolescents question their parents' authority and decisions (Berk, 2001).

As *Diversity Issue 2.1* indicates, young adolescents and their educators often deal with unplanned pregnancies. In fact, 26,000 females under the age of 15 experienced pregnancy in 1996; of these, approximately 10,000 had induced abortions (U.S. Bureau of the Census, 2000). These unplanned pregnancies and child rearing often lead to negative health outcomes, financial hardships, and in some cases, ineffective parenting (Papalia, Olds, & Feldman, 2001). Although Belgrave, Van Oss Marin, and Chambers (2000) focused only on African American girls, the problem of unplanned pregnancies affects young adolescents of all cultures.

Diversity Issue 2.1
Risky Sexual Attitudes Among Urban African American Girls in Early Adolescence

Belgrave, Van Oss Marin, and Chambers (2000) investigated the role of cultural factors in explaining the sexual attitudes among African American urban girls, ages 10-13. The authors reported disturbing findings: African American teenagers constitute only 14 percent of the adolescent population, yet account for 29 percent of all adolescent births. Early sexual activity increases the risk of STDs and HIV; contributes to lower academic success; limits vocational and career plans; and often results in family conflicts, peer difficulties, lowered self-esteem, depression, and various emotional problems. The authors studied school achievement, family cohesion, religiosity, and self-esteem. They found that African American girls who scored higher on these variables endorsed less risky sexual attitudes.

Their findings included:

- Factors affecting early sexual activity include family and community, self-esteem and locus of control, peer and interpersonal relationships, and school interest and achievement.
- Schools with high academic achievement are more likely to have resources to promote values and behaviors that counter risky sexual attitudes and other problem behaviors.
- Family structure was only marginally significant (i.e., it is not clear whether being in a two-parent versus one-parent household has an influence on sexual attitudes).
- Religiosity was not a significant predictor of risky sexual practices.
- Girls with higher self-esteem reported less risky sexual attitudes.

Middle school educators undoubtedly need to promote self-esteem and to plan developmentally appropriate health and sex education for young females of all cultures.

Source: Belgrave, F. Z., Van Oss Marin, N., & Chambers, D. B. (2000). Cultural, contextual, and intrapersonal predictors of risky sexual attitudes among urban African American girls in early adolescence. *Cultural Diversity and Ethnic Minority Psychology, 6*(3), 309-322.

Physical Development: Implications for Middle Level School Educators

Knowledge of young adolescents' developmental characteristics contributes to understanding their behavior and planning developmentally appropriate middle level schools. Research on physical development uncovered several implications for educators working with young adolescents.

First, educators should respond appropriately to 10- to 15-year-olds' concerns about developmental differences. Schools should examine practices and expectations that ignore variability in maturation, such as chronological age or ability grouping for all activities. For example, the tremendous physical differences among many 13-year-old boys can lead to significant problems for late maturers, in terms of not only physical strength and stamina, but also psychosocial development. Activities that stress strength and stamina and lead to unfavorable comparisons should be de-emphasized.

In a soccer game, a nearly fully developed 13-year-old boy outplayed and outmaneuvered another boy of the same age. A perceptive teacher, understanding how the smaller boy felt, responded by talking with him and, eventually, making arrangements for two soccer teams. Thus, late developers could have better feelings about their size, stamina, and strength.

Second, educators can respond appropriately to 10- to 15-year-olds' concerns about the onset of puberty and developing sexuality. Young adolescents need to understand the changes occurring in their bodies and know which changes are normal and expected (and, of course, recognize those changes that warrant medical attention). Judy Blume's (1970) book *Are You There, God? It's Me, Margaret* presented a situation in which a girl wondered why her menstrual period had not yet begun. Both boys and girls need to learn that while the sequence of development remains the same, rates among various boys and girls may differ significantly.

Third, curricular and instructional design should address 10- to 15-year-olds' need for movement and exercise, as well as their concern with body image and

---

Chart 2.2
Physical Development:
Implications for Middle Level Educators

Physical Development and Its Effects
- Understand how physical diversity affects psychosocial development (e.g., its effects on self-esteem and socialization)
- Teach young adolescents that development occurs at varying rates, and slow or late development should not cause alarm

Developmentally Appropriate Physical Activities
- Avoid competition between early and late maturing students
- Avoid expecting young adolescents to perform athletic activities for which they lack the stamina and muscular strength

Healthful Living
- Offer educational experiences in nutrition, healthful living, proper exercise, and adequate health
- Provide developmentally appropriate instruction on drug use, pregnancy, AIDS, and sexually transmitted diseases

Active Learning
- Provide educational experiences that allow active participation (e.g., independent study, community service, role playing, and experimentation), rather than long periods of passive sitting
- Take advantage of learning centers that promote student involvement and collaboration

Accurate Sources of Information
- Encourage young adolescents to consult parents, teachers, counselors, and school nurses for accurate answers to questions
- Provide educational experiences (direct instruction, exploratory programs, and adviser-advisee programs) that teach young adolescents about their changing bodies. (Manning & Bucher, 2001)

---

perceived attractiveness (Jackson & Davis, 2000). The awkwardness and discomfort associated with changing bodies, including lack of coordination, should be considered when planning classroom organization. Young adolescents need sufficient opportunities to stretch and walk around, desks and seating arrangements appropriate for growing bodies, and sufficient room between rows so legs and arms can be extended without disrupting other students. One middle level school provided different size desks, rather than expecting all learners to fit into the one desk style assigned to that grade. Educators allowed students to walk around the room during designated times. Even during periods of direct instruction, teachers provided "stretch breaks" during which young adolescents could move around the room.

Fourth, as young adolescents develop physically, they are more prone to depression, withdrawal, self-injurious behaviors, physical complaints, illegal actions, running away, and substance abuse (Papalia, Olds, & Feldman, 2001). Middle level educators need to be on the lookout for such symptoms and be prepared to address the problems either through developmentally appropriate curricular experiences or an adviser-advisee program.

One 8th-grade boy who had struggled academically for years began to complain of physical ailments, such as headaches and stomach pains. Some days he looked (perhaps unknowingly) for reasons to stay home; other days, he went to school and did little academic work. He seemed to withdraw from his friends. These were evident signs of depression. The team leader mentioned the problem to the guidance counselor, who promised to include his name on her already too-long list of students to see. Unfortunately, in this case, little was done to help a student who was obviously experiencing problems. Chart 2.2 summarizes some physical development and implications for middle level schools.

Psychosocial Development

Psychosocial Characteristics of Young Adolescents

Psychosocial development can be defined as the growth and development of young adolescents' psychological, social, and emotional domains such as socialization, self-esteem, and friendships (Manning & Bucher, 2001). Social and emotional growth for young adolescents is characterized by positive encounters as well as frustration, anger, and perceived social failure (Brown, 2001). Young adolescents experience these psychosocial developmental changes as they progress toward the adolescent years. Educators acquainted with young adolescents can attest to the fact that considerable diversity exists. Some young adolescents are outgoing and socially oriented, while others are self-conscious and painfully shy. While specific psychosocial characteristics can be identified, considerable variability exists as to when individual 10- to 15-year-olds demonstrate these characteristics.

A 7th-grade teacher had a painfully shy student in his class. While he spoke to the girl every morning, she never offered a verbal response. Her only acknowledgment was a hint of a smile. She rarely said anything to anyone, including the girls who sat beside her. About four months into the school year, the teacher asked the class a question and her hand went up! The teacher, obviously surprised, called on her and praised her correct answer. For the remainder of the year, however, she continued to be quiet and usually spoke only when necessary.

Characteristic 1. Young adolescents make friends and interact socially, a characteristic crucial to psychosocial development.

Making friends and gaining peer approval become especially important as young adolescents develop psychosocially. Peer interaction and friendships serve especially important functions during this period as boys and girls adjust to the physical and emotional changes of puberty. Friendships, positive peer relationships, and social interaction can boost young adolescents' self-esteem. Other benefits include reduced anxiety as trust and respect build a reinforced sense of identity, and development of interpersonal skills important for future interpersonal relationships.

Close friendships begin to emerge during the first or middle stages of early adolescence. Young adolescents see friends on a daily basis and develop a system of cliques, defined as "small groups of about five to seven members who are good friends and . . . resemble one another in family background, attitudes, and values" (Berk, 2001, p. 404). Boys tend to congregate in groups and have a fairly extensive network of friends, while girls are more likely to form one or two close friendships with other girls. During these years, young adolescents more readily share their inner thoughts and feelings and disclose personal information with friends.

Since early adolescence is a crucial period for identity formation, gender differences in friendships and peer relations should be understood and addressed. Girls during the early teen years have personal conversations with friends more often, confide in a friend more often, and report more self-disclosure than boys do. Other gender differences include: boys have larger social networks than girls, males concern themselves with attributes construed to be important for status in the peer group, and girls demonstrate more concern with attributes necessary for relationships with a few friends (Benenson, 1990). Friendships during early adolescence occur mostly between same-sex friends, while cross-sex friendships begin later. As *Diversity Issue 2.2* shows, however, friendship decisions might differ with sexual orientation, which "appears to be influenced by an interaction of biological and environmental factors and may be at least partly genetic" (Papalia, Olds, & Feldman, 2001, p. 479). Lesbian and gay students during this developmental period often report feeling different, confused about role and sexual identity, unsure about whether to tell others, and rejected by peers (Berk, 2001).

Diversity Issue 2.2
Lesbian and Gay Young Adolescents

Howard Taylor encouraged middle school educators to address the needs of lesbian and gay young adolescents, a group he thinks experiences at-risk conditions and behaviors such as truancy, dropping out, suicide, drug and alcohol abuse, sexual abuse, and AIDS.

Taylor maintained that lesbian and gay young adolescents often feel "different" (p. 221) from their same-sex peers. Taylor emphasizes that while feeling different does not necessarily mean a child is lesbian or gay, such feelings might be the first stage in the development of a lesbian or gay identity. As children start to develop same-sex attractions, they may engage in same-sex sexual behaviors and begin to consider themselves lesbian or gay. At the same time as these children begin suspecting they are lesbian or gay, they also realize that society expects them to be heterosexual. The expectation is clear: there are few (if any) lesbian or gay role models, family members may reject nonconforming children, and classmates may launch verbal and physical attacks.

Strategies offered by Taylor include integrating relevant information into the curriculum, discussing injustices and discrimination lesbians and gays receive, and using books with lesbian and gay themes. In closing, Taylor proposed middle school educators should work toward a school climate that fosters warmth, care, and respect for all young adolescents, including those who are lesbian or gay.

Source: Taylor, H. E. (2000). Meeting the needs of lesbian and gay young adolescents. *The Clearing House, 73*(4), 221-224.

The young adolescent who lags in psychosocial development or who lacks age-appropriate social skills often misses out on many learning and social opportunities and, in some ways, fails to achieve or satisfy crucial developmental tasks for this period. These young adolescents are found in all middle schools; their situation may be the result of family problems, a lack of interpersonal skills, some emotional disorder, or simply a lack of psychosocial development. While identifying the reason is important, it is just as important for middle level educators to take action to help students develop appropriate social skills and to promote their self-esteem.

Children rejected by their peers often report feelings of loneliness and lower levels of self-esteem. Educators need to be aware of rejected and friendless students and carefully assess these individual situations. Such assessment should begin by asking:

- Do children in the class avoid, ignore, or reject the child?
- Is the child bullied or harassed for a specific reason (e.g., a disabling condition, lagging physical development, unwillingness to defend oneself, sexual orientation, or choice of clothes)?
- Does the child lack social skills necessary for successful interaction with others?
- Does the child have difficulty communicating with others?
- Does the child act aggressively while interacting with others?
- Does the child disrupt others in the class?

Perceptive middle level educators realize the importance of friendships, and so make a deliberate effort to help social isolates and those being bullied or harassed. Accepting such a responsibility is a major task, especially when one considers the long-term consequences of not having friends.

Teachers also notice rapidly changing friendships among young adolescents. A best friend one day might be an enemy tomorrow and vice-versa. During early February, a 13-year-old girl enthusiastically planned her mid-March birthday party. She said, "I have all my plans made except who to invite." Her father asked why she could not make her guest list then. The young girl responded, "But, Dad, I don't know who I will be friends with at that time!"

Characteristic 2. *Young adolescents shift their allegiance and affiliation from parents and teachers toward the peer group, which becomes the prime source for standards and models of behavior.*

Developmentally, young adolescents become socially curious and demonstrate increased social interactions and consciousness. While they continue to value family members, they begin to reach outside their family for social experiences, companionship, and approval. Contact with parents begins to decrease and the nature of social interactions gradually changes. Parents and teachers during these times may feel that they have less influence.

Peers assume central importance (Papalia, Olds, & Feldman, 2001) and have a tremendous influence on the behavior, speech, dress, and grooming of young adolescents (Berk, 2001). During these times, middle level educators should perceive peer pressure as a vital aspect of the socialization process. Trying to compete with a young adolescent's peers can be a difficult process.

Young adolescents become increasingly aware of their own selves and their relationships with peers. The peer group often serves as the primary reference source for attitudes, values, and behavior and provides a mechanism for decision-making. Even without overt changes in behavior, peers' values become powerful forces in a child's actions and overall behavior. In some cases, the 10- to 15-year-old believes that maintaining allegiance to parents and teachers can result in loss of peer approval and acceptance.

Parents are often upset when their children begin to shift their allegiance to peers. One mother said, "I do not know what happened to Nicole. All of a sudden, she changed. Instead of listening to us, she started listening to that group of friends she hangs around with. I think she looks for reasons to get out of the house." The teacher tried to explain that although such behavior is disturbing, it is expected during the early adolescence developmental period. She added that while Nicole was looking for freedom and wanted to affiliate with peers, she still needed to know her teachers and parents were available to play significant roles in her life.

Characteristic 3. *Young adolescents' preoccupation with themselves leads to an examination of all aspects of their development and overall "self."*

A preoccupation with oneself naturally develops during this period. Young adolescents constantly examine their physical and social characteristics and compare themselves to others of similar age and developmental levels. Youngsters with overt height, weight, and related differences may be the only ones to notice such differences, which can have a significant effect on their perceptions of themselves. This characteristic plays a significant role in young adolescents' lives because self-perceptions influence their opinion of their abilities to interact socially.

Both girls and boys often look in the mirror in an effort to determine the "normalcy" of their development. In their preoccupation with themselves, they compare themselves with others and what they *think* they should be and should look like. Their conclusions about their development and themselves in general have significant influences on their decisions about peers, friendships, and behavioral choices.

Characteristic 4. *Young adolescents increasingly seek freedom and independence from adult authority*.

While young adolescents spend an increasing amount of time with peers, in most cases, relationships with parents and families continue to be close and influential (Papalia, Olds, & Feldman, 2001). Still, the quest for independence and autonomy plays a powerful role during early adolescence. These youngsters expend considerable energy to move toward greater control over their lives and increased freedom from authority. Serious examination of long-held beliefs and allegiances begins to occur, often resulting in a move toward greater independence and freedom from authority figures (George & Alexander, 1993).

In their search for independence, young adolescents may rebuke authority; engage in vandalism; or become involved with sex, alcohol, or drugs. Although some may not even want to participate in such activities, being actively involved promotes a sense of freedom from adult authority and a sense of allegiance to peers. Social changes (resulting from new ways of thinking, feeling, and acting) allow reflection upon social experiences. These social changes, accompanied by physical and emotional changes associated with puberty, sometimes result in behaviors that educators and parents find unusual and disturbing.

Characteristic 5. *Young adolescents experience changing self-esteem, which is influenced by all aspects of their lives—both at home and at school—as well as by peers, who continually test self-worth* (Papalia, Olds, & Feldman, 2001).

Many young adolescents experience an adjusting self-esteem that may fluctuate daily or with any given situation. Moving to a new school where they no longer reign as the oldest and biggest, young adolescents must reassess their standing with both peers and teachers. The transition from elementary to middle level school is a stressful time (McElroy, 2000) that can have a long-lasting and negative impact on young adolescents' self-esteem.

As young adolescents' self-esteem constantly changes, this is certainly a time when middle level educators should provide stability and security (e.g., continued indicators of acceptance, familiar school routines, and emphasis on physical and psychological safety). These efforts can contribute to young adolescents' normal development and self-esteem.

While observers of young adolescents have long thought that rapidly changing physical developments had corresponding effects on psychosocial development, one study documented a significant relationship among gender differences, self-esteem, and body image and offered other observations. Several generalizations concerning gender differences can be made:

- Males feel more satisfied with their bodies than females do.
- Males, rating some aspects of their bodies positively, were more likely to rate most aspects similarly; females, on the other hand, assigned different values to different aspects of their bodies.
- Changes affecting the female body have the potential to make the girl disappointed in her body, while the male may be more concerned with task mastery and effectiveness than with physical appearance. (Koff, Rierdan, & Stubbs, 1990)

Selected Psychosocial Theorists: Erikson and Havighurst

Erik Erikson (1963) and Robert Havighurst (1972) both proposed developmental stage theories. Erikson focused on psychosocial stages, while Havighurst focused on developmental tasks. Since they proposed their theories prior to the acceptance of early adolescence as a distinct developmental stage, neither discussed stages specifically for young adolescents. Still, middle level educators can use their theories to identify age-appropriate psychosocial stages and developmental tasks.

Erikson's Psychosocial Theories. Humans develop through eight psychosocial stages, with each having an age range and distinct characteristics (Erikson, 1963). As previously mentioned, Erikson did not designate a distinct 10- to 15-year-old age range. Neither did he consider the influence of cultural and gender differences on psychosocial crises. In fact, readers should be aware that some find Erikson's model to be biased to the point of excluding females' developmental process (Rice, 2001). Early adolescence actually crosses two of Erikson's psychosocial stages: Industry vs. Inferiority (6 to 11 years) and Identity vs. Role Confusion (12 to 18 years) (Berk, 2001; Papalia, Olds, & Feldman, 2001).

Erikson viewed the Industry vs. Inferiority stage (6 to 11 years) as a time when intellect and performance dominate learners' behavior. Children basically form an opinion of themselves as either "industrious" or "inferior." During this stage, learners need to accomplish specific and worthwhile tasks, complete all assignments, and feel a sense of pride.

Young adolescents next pass through the Identity vs. Role Confusion stage (12 to 18 years). Learners seek an identity by striving for increased independence from adults and by concerning themselves with the kind of person they are becoming. The need for independence and peer acceptance grows during this stage as students seek a sense of self.

Depending upon development, young adolescents, usually considered to be 10- to 15-year-olds, experience some crises in both the Industry vs. Inferiority stage and the Identity vs. Role Confusion stage. Using Erikson's psychosocial theories as a basis, middle level educators can provide developmentally appropriate curricular and instructional practices that:

- Recognize skills, abilities, and accomplishments
- Understand the influence of peers and "positive" peer pressure
- Offer opportunities for learners to identify positively with peers and achieve feelings of adequacy
- Provide appropriate learning experiences that address psychosocial changes
- Understand cliques as part of life
- Understand how behavior affects others
- Understand the significance of increased independence and responsibility
- Understand the need to search for ideals, yet maintain a sense of reality.

Havighurst's Developmental Tasks. Havighurst (1972) proposed a social stage theory that divides a person's life into six developmental stages. He offered the following definition:

> A developmental task is a task which arises at or about a certain time in the life of an individual, successful achievement of which leads to his happiness and to success with later tasks, while failure leads to unhappiness in the individual, disapproval by the society, and difficulty with later tasks. (Havighurst, 1972, p. 2)

Understanding developmental tasks, or those major common tasks that all individuals must confront, can be helpful when predicting physical, psychosocial, and intellectual challenges facing young adolescents. Developmental tasks appropriate for young adolescents include: 1) achieving new and more mature relations with age-mates of both sexes, 2) continuing to learn an appropriate gender role, 3) beginning to achieve emotional independence from parents and other adults, and 4) working toward socially responsible behavior.

Middle level school educators need to select age-appropriate developmental tasks from the later years of the 6 to 12 period (i.e., 10 to 12) and the beginning years (or 12 to 15) of the adolescent stage. Havighurst's theories support the importance of encouraging young adolescents to:

- Understand how a healthy identity enhances one's coping strategies for personal problem-solving abilities (Rice, 2001)
- Learn social skills and listen to and consider differing viewpoints
- Develop values and a sense of morality as cognitive abilities and moral judgments assume more complexity (Papalia, Olds, & Feldman, 2001)
- Begin development of independence
- Develop positive attitudes toward varying social groups and institutions
- Recognize the influence of peer groups
- Develop satisfying social contacts and understand democratic procedures
- Understand and accept bodies, recognizing tremendous variability and normal changes
- Be responsible for behavior in home, school, and community
- Understand how one's behavior affects others.

To help young adolescents meet these tasks, educators should recognize the influence of peer pressure and changing allegiances, and encourage the beginning stages of emotional independence. They should teach students to be responsible for their own behavior, both at school and home, and continue to teach social skills necessary for getting along with age-mates.

Psychosocial Development: Implications for Middle Level School Educators

Changing social characteristics during early adolescence can have a profound impact on both young adolescents and their teachers. These psychosocial changes have important implications for middle level educators in terms of friendships, self-esteem, peer pressure, school climate, academic achievement, and teaching and learning practices.

First, middle level educators can provide appropriate opportunities for social interaction and friendship building. While young adolescents wanting to work alone should be given the opportunity to do so, educators also should encourage learners to interact in socially oriented situations, cooperative work groups, mini-courses, exploratory programs, and adviser-advisee groups. One middle level teacher allowed students to choose their learning groups and encouraged social interaction through breaks and participation in clubs and extracurricular activities.

Second, educators need to understand and accept 10- to 15-year-olds' natural shift in allegiance from parents and teachers to peers and friends. This shifting of allegiance, accompanied by peer pressure, becomes a powerful influence on young adolescents' socialization. Effective middle level teachers accept the futility of trying to compete with learners' peers for allegiance, and work within the confines of young adolescents' shifting allegiances.

Third, examining one's changing body is another natural aspect of early adolescence. A nose that appears to be crooked, feet that are perceived as too big, a lack of coordination, feelings of anonymity, and a host of other concerns can result in critical self-examination and shattered self-esteem. One 14-year-old confided to her family that she thought her nose was too big. After the family assured her that her nose was not too big, she left the room only to return soon to announce, "My feet are too big!" Her next concern was that she was "too tall." Her family tried, but failed, to convince the young girl that her nose, feet, and height were not abnormal.

Teachers of 10- to 15-year-olds should encourage a realistic self-appraisal. An interdisciplinary team at one middle level school includes self-evaluation in its adviser-advisee sessions and exploratory activities. Teachers examine developmental topics and convey to young adolescents that developmental rates and differences are normal. They provide opportunities for students to learn about changing bodies, to know the difference between normal and abnormal development, and to avoid being too critical of themselves or others.

Fourth, young adolescents' quest for freedom and independence needs to be understood in its developmental context. They are too old to require constant care, yet too young to achieve the independence of adolescents. Responding to this desire for increased freedom and independence, educators can provide learners with opportunities to engage in decision-making. Possible strategies include allowing students the freedom to make significant decisions about their school day or to work independently.

This quest for freedom and independence also demands a degree of responsibility. Young adolescents need opportunities to behave responsibly and to demonstrate their growing capacity for self-control and self-management in safe and psychologically secure settings.

Fifth, and critical to all aspects of young adolescents' development, middle level educators need to respond appropriately to youngsters' changing self-esteems. Self-

---

Chart 2.3
Psychosocial Development: Implications for Middle Level Educators

Friendships and Peers
- Understand the importance of friendships to positive psychosocial development and provide opportunities for young adolescents to make friends
- Understand the difficulty of teachers and parents competing with peers, yet continue to influence young adolescents in positive and constructive ways

Self-Esteem
- Understand that self-esteem affects nearly all aspects of development
- Provide direct opportunities through curricular experiences, organizational patterns, instructional approaches, exploratory programs, and adviser-advisee programs to build self-esteem

Allegiance and Affiliation
- Teach young adolescents that shifting allegiances are normal developmental occurrences for which they should feel neither guilty nor uncomfortable
- Help young adolescents understand that pursuits of freedom should not lead to dangerous or unsafe practices (i.e., freedom requires responsibility)

Gender Differences
- Recognize gender differences in socialization and friendship formation while carefully avoiding stereotypical generalizations
- Plan gender-responsive social opportunities (e.g., opportunities for more collaboration and less competition)

Socialization and Social Tasks
- Provide educational experiences (e.g., role playing) that teach young adolescents how to handle social tasks
- Encourage debates and other outlets for young adolescents to be argumentative in a socialized manner. (Manning & Bucher, 2001)

esteem may vary due to skin problems, lack of coordination, or feelings of anonymity in a large middle level school. A teacher's comment may have no visible impact one day, while the next day the same comment may reduce a young adolescent to tears.

Chart 2.3 provides readers with a look at selected psychosocial developmental characteristics and implications for developmentally appropriate educational practices.

Case Study 2.1
Developmental Portrait of a 12-Year-Old Girl

J.L.M. is a 12-year-old in the middle of the early adolescence developmental period. She is a 6th-grader in a medium-size middle level school. An energetic cheerleader, she plays tennis, swims, plays the clarinet, and is an officer in the "Just Say No" club. J.L.M. thinks she is pretty, but worries about the size of her nose. She enjoys attending school and likes writing; however, she is not particularly interested in the academic areas of school. In fact, her teachers and parents must continually encourage her to keep up with her schoolwork. She likes to read, but her grades do not always reflect her ability.

J.L.M. is growing taller and heavier, developing facial and bodily features that indicate she is approaching adolescence. Hair is appearing on her arms and legs. Although menstruation has not yet begun, both she and her parents know the time is near.

While her friendships change often, J.L.M. usually has one or two close friends at a time. What her friends think and their perceptions of her are crucial. Her choice of a hairstyle, shoes, and notebook often depends on her choice of friends. She constantly examines her appearance, clothes, and mannerisms. Seeking independence from her parents and extending allegiance to her friends, she is far more concerned about her friends' perceptions than her parents'. Her self-esteem fluctuates. One day, she feels good about her appearance and her ability to cope with both school and home, while on another day she considers herself to be the world's doormat.

No longer confined to thinking in concrete terms, J.L.M. is developing the ability to think abstractly and critically. She thinks about thinking, analyzes and synthesizes data, poses questions to herself and others, and offers strategies and solutions to problems. Her cognitive development is satisfactory, yet she is bothered when she cannot perform all the mental operations that other students can. She responds quickly to intellectual stimulation and is usually ready to be challenged. She also enjoys working cooperatively with her friends in intellectual pursuits.

Overall, J.L.M. is a happy young adolescent. She has friends, feels competent, and enjoys the social aspects of school. She realizes she is developing and, while these changes often lead to questions, she feels good about herself, her life, and her prospects for the future.

Cognitive Development

Cognitive Characteristics of Young Adolescents

Just as with physical and psychosocial developmental characteristics, young adolescents have their own unique cognitive developmental characteristics. Cognitive development can be defined as the changes and advancements that occur in intellectual or cognitive skills—for example, the ability to learn, think, and reason (Manning & Bucher, 2001). This section looks at selected cognitive characteristics and implications for educational practice.

Characteristic 1. Young adolescents' development progresses from Piaget's concrete operations stage to the formal operations stage.

During the concrete operations stage, young adolescents have the ability to think out problems. This ability includes classification, organizing objects into a series, and reversing operations. Specifically, the young adolescent masters logical operations using material with concrete content and thinks in concrete terms about a problem. The young adolescent understands principles of conservation, uses various approaches to solving a problem, understands the relationship of the parts to the whole, and performs the operation of serializing. Language becomes primarily sociocentric, while egocentric speech decreases (Ginsburg & Opper, 1988).

As development progresses and young adolescents begin functioning in the formal operations stage, several characteristics become evident: comprehension of abstract concepts (e.g., ability to form "ideas" and reason about the future), ability to handle contrary-to-fact propositions, and ability to develop and test hypotheses. In the early stages, the learner may make correct discoveries and handle certain formal operations, yet is unable to provide systematic and rigorous proof. Later, the learner formulates more sophisticated generalizations, reasoning, and proofs (Ginsburg & Opper, 1988).

Considerable research evidence contradicts the belief that the formal operations stage of thinking begins around age 11 or 12 (Berk, 2001). As emphasized in Chapter 3, one simply cannot assume all young adolescents have developed into Piaget's formal operations stage. Some young adolescents continue to function in the concrete operations stage. Rather than basing education decisions on erroneous assumptions, educators must assess young adolescents individually to determine whether they have progressed to the formal operations stage or continue to function in the concrete operations stage.

Characteristic 2. Young adolescents experience gradual changes in thinking that result in considerable diversity in their development.

Gradual cognitive changes mean that learners think abstractly and reflectively in one area and in concrete terms in another area. For example, young adolescents may offer perceptive and thoughtful comments about social justice, yet at the same time may be unable to master concepts requiring logic and high-level thinking. In any event, immature thinking persists in some attitudes and behaviors (Papalia, Olds, & Feldman, 2001).

While physical and psychosocial diversity can be readily detected, the more abstract nature of thinking and thought often leads educators to assume all learners are functioning on a similar cognitive level. Another serious error occurs when teachers assume that a learner functioning on a high or low level in one cognitive area also functions at a similar level in another area.

Gender differences, either biologically or socially based (or perhaps both), appear in intellectual abilities during early adolescence. Prior to puberty, both boys and girls show little or no difference in measures of verbal and spatial abilities. After puberty, however, girls score higher on verbal measures and boys score higher on spatial ability measures. Middle level educators should avoid contributing to these differences by advising both boys and girls to pursue similar areas (Butler & Manning, 1998).

Characteristic 3. *Young adolescents begin to think hypothetically, abstractly, reflectively, and critically.*

Young adolescents experience a rapid unfolding of cognitive capacities. They begin to think reflectively and to think about thinking. This newfound ability opens the door to more complex and abstract thought processes. This period of cognitive development also provides opportunities for higher levels of intellectual thought and effective communication. During this period, young adolescents develop the ability to analyze and synthesize data; grasp complex scientific principles; pose questions, explore, experiment, and reason; grapple with social and political issues; and apply different strategies and solutions to problems (Berk, 2001).

Questioning rules, thinking about the future, commitment to abstract ideals, excitement about learning new concepts, and diminution of egocentrism characterize development of advanced thinking abilities (Berk, 2001). However, as previously stated, young adolescents differ greatly. Some young adolescents need opportunities for concrete thinking and experiences, while others need opportunities to experiment with their new abstract reasoning skills. In some cases, young adolescents might need both, depending on individual abilities in various areas.

Characteristic 4. *Young adolescents begin to develop the ability to make reasoned moral and ethical choices.*

Piaget (1948) believed that intellectual and moral growth correspond, and proposed that children between the ages of 9 and 11 develop the ability to internalize the rightness and wrongness of situations. Developing from the concrete operations to the formal operations stage, young adolescents can reason about the morality of a situation. Likewise, they are more inquisitive, more assertive, and employ personal curiosity to test and determine the moral and ethical validity of ideas.

Young adolescents' ability to think hypothetically, abstractly, and reflectively and to make reasoned or ethical choices depends upon their level of cognitive development. All learners do not develop at the same rate. Learners continuing to function in the concrete operations stage may be unable to participate in activities with those learners who are functioning in Piaget's formal operations stage.

The early adolescence years are crucial times for forming lifelong self-esteem and identities (Davis, 1993). While middle level educators must use caution in teaching values, Davis suggested four general goals of values training and moral development. Students need to: 1) be consciously aware of constructive values and behaviors, 2) think logically about the consequences of bad attitudes and bad behavior, 3) empathize with victims of negative behavior, and 4) make personal commitments to constructive values and behavior.

To address these four general goals, Davis (1993) suggested several exercises for young adolescents. First, asking such questions as "Why is it important to be honest?" (p. 32) helps young adolescents to understand a value and its related behavior. Second, analogical thinking such as "How is a good person like a good pizza?" (p. 33) makes students think and formulate plausible explanations. Third, the empathy approach involves students by asking, for example, how someone might feel when her birthday gift is stolen the day after she receives it. Fourth, questioning and discussion approaches elicit awareness and commitment (e.g., asking students whether a good person considers others' feelings).

Selected Cognitive Theorists: Piaget and Gardner

Many theorists have contributed to the understanding of cognitive development and to educators' ability to provide appropriate educational experiences. Because of limited space, this section looks at only two: one old (Piaget's developmental stages) and one relatively new (Gardner's multiple intelligences). Both Piaget's and Gardner's contributions have implications for middle level educators.

Piaget's Developmental Stages. Piaget theorized that maturing children pass through four developmental stages: sensory-motor (birth to 2), preoperational (2 to 7), concrete operational (7 to 12), and formal operational (12 and beyond). Although variability exists in the beginning and duration of developmental stages, he maintained that the stages occur in a constant, invariant sequence, with each stage having educational significance. Developmental stages having the most relevance for middle level educators include the concrete operations stage (7 to 12) and the formal operations stage (12 and beyond).

The concrete operations stage exemplifies the child's ability to see relationships, move from deductive to inductive thinking, and initiate logical thinking processes. In this stage, learners cannot deal consistently and effectively with abstractions or generalizations. The concrete operations stage corresponds closely to the late elementary and beginning middle level school years (Ginsburg & Opper, 1988).

The formal operations stage exemplifies the child's capacity to conceptualize abstract relationships, employ inductive thinking, and expand logical thinking processes. During this stage, learners consider all aspects of a problem and experiment, hypothesize, and analyze to arrive at conclusions.

Most young adolescents function in a transitory stage between Piaget's concrete operational and formal operational stages. The learner's cognitive development includes the ability to organize information around categories or concepts, which allows for generalizations and contributes to increasingly higher levels of cognitive functioning. Likewise, some learners demonstrate early formal operations characteristics such as comprehension of concepts, reasoning about the future, ability to handle contrary-to-fact propositions, and ability to test hypotheses (Ginsburg & Opper, 1988). While they are expected to function at the formal operations stage, most young adolescents have difficulty with abstract tasks and, therefore, still function as concrete thinkers.

Gardner's Multiple Intelligences. Understanding the theory of multiple intelligences requires a brief review of traditional perspectives on intelligence. Intelligence traditionally has been defined as the ability to solve problems or create culturally valued products (Papalia, Olds, & Feldman, 2001). Also, traditional definitions contend that one's general intelligence, an inborn attribute, does not change significantly with age or with training and experience. The theory of multiple intelligences challenges the prevailing concept of intelligence as an individual's single general capacity. Instead, it proposes a number of different intelligences rather than one overall intelligence.

Gardner (1993) believes that learners have at least seven intelligences:

- Logical mathematical: enjoy solving problems, finding patterns, outlining, calculating
- Linguistic: relate to the meaning, rhythms, and sounds of words
- Spatial: like to design, invent, imagine, and create
- Bodily kinesthetic: learn through physical movement, mimicking, and touching
- Musical/rhythmic: enjoy the human voice, and respond to environmental and instructional sounds
- Interpersonal: can understand the feelings of others
- Intrapersonal: understand own emotions, motivations, and moods.

The theory of multiple intelligences can help teachers actively involve students in learning experiences, develop particular intelligences that teachers think students lack (yet are important for life success), and design culturally responsive approaches to reach learners who have trouble learning. Chart 2.4 shows an example of a four-week unit on the 1920s that pertains to different learning styles.

Cognitive Development: Implications for Middle Level School Educators

Young adolescents' cognitive abilities can provide a basis for planning middle level teaching and learning experiences.

First, Piaget's ideas on cognitive development can be a valuable resource. Rather than assuming that young adolescents function in the concrete operations stage or the formal operations stage, teachers need to assess individual students' levels of thought prior to reaching curricular and instructional decisions, thus ensuring developmental appropriateness. Learning requires that children be given the opportunity to manipulate and think about objects and to develop process skills. Also, young adolescents who are preoccupied with non-school matters need sufficient motivation to hold their attention.

Two middle school authorities (George & Alexander, 1993) suggest that great

Chart 2.4
Multiple Intelligences

This 4-week unit for the 7th grade shows how multiple intelligences can be used to teach students about the 1920s. The following are examples of activities within the unit that reflect multiple intelligences.

Linguistic
- Interview people who lived in the town during the 1920s. If possible, locate pictures and/or postcards to show how the town looked, and then prepare a written description.
- Use a desktop publishing program to create a newspaper featuring information about the 1920s, such as the death of Floyd Collins and the Scopes trial in Tennessee.

Spatial
- Identify the major events of the 1920s and create a time line.
- Research people, such as Jessie Redmond Faussett, Walter White, Zora Neal Hurston, Langston Hughes, and Countee Cullen, who made literary and artistic contributions during the Harlem Renaissance. Using a map of New York City, pinpoint key places where literary and artistic accomplishments occurred.

Interpersonal
- Work in cooperative learning groups to discuss several government scandals that began during President Harding's administration, such as the Teapot Dome Scandal and the one involving Continental Trading Company.
- Select four or five famous people from the 1920s and have them "appear" on a panel to discuss their contributions. Make a list of guidelines to help students maintain positive rapport with other panel members.

Intrapersonal
- Share feelings and impressions about the "Roaring Twenties" with other students. Were these positive or negative times in which to live? Why?
- Select a person from the "Roaring Twenties" and research her or his life. Step into that person's shoes and compare her or his life with your life today.

Kinesthetic
- Learn dances popular in the 1920s and try to show how the movements reflect the perspectives of the time period.
- Produce a short video using the format of a "you were there" look at history.

numbers of students remain in the concrete operations stage throughout their middle school years. Learners in the concrete operations stage may be unable to generalize broad contexts (i.e., to hypothesize from existing facts). These learners may have difficulty dealing effectively with the past in a realistically chronological manner. They may be unable to reverse mental operations or consider situations that appear contrary to personal observations. Teaching a class with students operating at the concrete level can be difficult, since most middle level school curricula have been designed to include hypothesizing, conceptualizing, and symbolizing. Providing diverse learning experiences with varied instructional strategies helps to communicate subject matter to students in either developmental stage (George & Alexander, 1993).

When planning specific experiences for young adolescents, middle level school educators should consider the following:

- Young adolescents in transition to the formal operations stage need opportunities to reason logically about verbal statements and with mathematical concepts such as permutations, combinations, probabilities, and correlations.
- Young adolescents need developmentally appropriate educational experiences that take advantage of their increasing ability to think abstractly, hypothetically, reflectively, and critically.
- Young adolescents' tremendous diversity requires that educators need to consider individual differences and varying levels of thinking ability, thus avoiding frustration among learners. One middle level teacher dealt with this diversity in two ways. First, she provided instruction on different levels. While some

students worked with concrete objects, others engaged in work requiring abstract thought. For example, some students worked on mathematics requiring several relatively clear steps and others worked on equations and probabilities. Second, she allowed students of varying abilities to work cooperatively toward a group goal. Students capable of higher level thinking assisted those who had not yet acquired such skills, subsequently explaining the rationale behind the thought process.

- Young adolescents need educators who recognize and address their multiple intelligences. While Susan has tremendous mathematics ability and should be encouraged to pursue her interest and expertise, Bill should be allowed to pursue music. One cannot assume that a learner with low intelligence in one area is not able to excel in another.

- Young adolescents benefit from opportunities to develop moral and ethical reasoning. The mission of developmentally appropriate middle level schools includes teaching young adolescents to think ethically; recognize good and bad; and embrace virtues such as courage, responsibility, honesty, integrity, tolerance, appreciation of individual differences, and caring for others (Jackson & Davis, 2000).

The issue of gender has received considerable attention (e.g., Butler & Manning, 1998) over the past several years. Some educators, when considering gender, focus primarily on issues affecting females. As Butler and Manning (1998) suggest, however, gender issues affect both girls and boys. *Diversity Issue 2.3* looks at a digest from the Women's Educational Equity Act Resource Center that stresses the importance of providing gender-equitable educational experiences, for both boys and girls.

Diversity Issue 2.3
What About the Boys?

In a somewhat controversial and debatable article, Kimmel (2000) reported that some authors (e.g., Christina Hoff Sommers, William Pollack, and Michael Thompson) perceive a "war against boys" (p. 1), in which boys are the "victims" of "misguided" feminist efforts to protect and promote girls' development. Nevertheless, Kimmel thinks that most middle class boys are taking their places in an unequal society to which they have always felt entitled.

Kimmel also maintained that the current discussion about where boys are and what they are doing encompasses three phenomena: numbers, achievement, and behavior. The data on boys seem to suggest that fewer and fewer boys are in school compared to girls, that boys are getting poorer grades, and that more boys are displaying behavioral problems. According to these critics, the salutary effects of paying attention to girls have been offset by increasing problems related to boys.

Kimmel proposed that both boys and girls experience gender inequality during adolescence. For example, girls suppress their ambition, while boys inflate ambition. Girls are more likely to undervalue their abilities, especially in the more traditional masculine subjects. Only the most able and most secure girls take mathematics and science courses. On the other hand, boys possess a false bravado and often face strong family pressure to *over-value* (italics Kimmel's) their abilities and, unlike girls, remain in programs in which they are less qualified and less able to succeed.

In the best possible scenario, gender-equitable education provides equal opportunities and enables each student to reach her or his potential. It reduces the gender disparities that are detrimental to classroom interactions; encourages all students to pursue a variety of school subjects, putting no limit on what they can accomplish; and gives students opportunities to participate in all aspects of the educational process.

Source: Kimmel, M. (2000, November). What about the boys? *Women's Educational Equity Act Center Digest,* 1-2, 7-8.

Just as with girls, boys and their gender-specific needs deserve to be recognized. Perceptive educators plan for boys' special gender issues (Pollack & Shuster, 2000), recognizing that many boys have a limited emotional repertoire for managing conflict, adversity, and change. Society and culture support emotional development for girls, yet usually discourage emotional development for boys (Thompson & Kindlon, 1999). Many boys feel sad, afraid, and angry, perhaps due to emotional training. Kindlon and Thompson (2000) maintain that the social and emotional challenges of school contribute to boys' emotional miseducation.

Chart 2.5 provides a summary of cognitive development and implications for developmentally appropriate education practice.

Case Study 2.2
Developmental Portrait of a 14–Year–Old Boy

M.P.M., a 13-year-old 7th-grader, attends a suburban middle level school that houses grades 6 to 8. He basically feels good about himself and his developing body, but he has questions about the changes that occur almost daily. M.P.M. is a good student. He does his homework and schoolwork, his teachers praise his behavior and grades, he participates in clubs and intramural soccer, and he serves as vice-president of the 7th-grade class. Basically, he has a good relationship with both his parents and teachers, yet increasingly values the opinions of his friends.

Physically, M.P.M. is growing larger and heavier. His arms, legs, shoulders, and thighs are showing signs of development. He can run faster and longer and can feel his overall strength increasing. He examines himself nearly every day and often compares his development to that of his friends, some of whom are larger and some smaller. He wants to grow and develop and improve his coordination, yet he wonders what he will look like when he grows up.

Chart 2.5
Cognitive Development:
Implications for Middle Level School Educators

Cognitive Diversity
- Consider young adolescents' varying cognitive development as well as their individual differences (e.g., varying attention spans, learning styles, multiple intelligences, and left brain/right brain capacities)
- Provide learning experiences that are appropriate for students' cognitive levels (e.g., use small-group instruction, select instructional materials for various reading and interest levels, and implement peer-tutoring and cross-age tutoring sessions)

Concrete and Formal Thinking
- Recognize that young adolescents do not reach the concrete and formal operations stage at the same time
- Provide formal operations thinkers with higher order thinking skills and cause-and-effect relationships, and provide concrete operational thinkers with manipulatives and non-abstract learnings

"Real-Life" Thinking
- Provide "real-life" thinking exercises in which young adolescents analyze and synthesize data and engage in experimentation and problem-solving
- Allow young adolescents to question school and home rules and to explore reasons for these rules

Changing Interests
- Recognize that young adolescents' cognitive interests are changing
- Adapt educational experiences to their changing interests

Ethics and Morality
- Understand and capitalize on the relationship between cognitive and moral development (i.e., higher order thinking skills allow higher levels of moral reasoning)
- Encourage young adolescents to consider the ethics and morality of social and personal situations, explore concepts of justice and equality, and consider such social issues as sexism, racism, and discrimination.

Source: Manning, M. L., & Bucher, K. T. (2001). *Teaching in the middle school.* Columbus, OH: Merrill/Prentice-Hall. Reprinted by permission.

Psychosocially, M.P.M. has a small group of friends (mostly of the same sex), interacts socially, and sees his friends daily. While M.P.M. abides by parental and teacher expectations, he is shifting his allegiance from the significant adults in his life to his friends. He increasingly wants independence and freedom. His self-concept fluctuates. Usually, he feels worthwhile, yet at times he questions his worth, his changing body, and what his future might bring.

Intellectually, M.P.M. is demonstrating an increasing ability to think reflectively and abstractly. His problem-solving ability is increasing and he successfully participates in problem-solving situations. He is developing a sense of morality and values, and realizes that issues cannot always be decided in black-and-white terms. Intellectually, M.P.M. is developing toward the formal operations stage: he can form "ideas" and reason about the future, handle contrary-to-fact propositions, and develop and test hypotheses.

M.P.M. basically feels good about himself, his increasing abilities, his school success, and his future. While he sometimes questions his lack of coordination and why some boys are larger and more coordinated, he feels pretty good about his development. Nevertheless, he sometimes goes to his social studies teacher for reassurance.

Concluding Remarks

Once considered only from a child or adolescent developmental perspective, young adolescents as a group have their own unique developmental period that is receiving wide recognition. Knowledge of young adolescents' developmental characteristics contributes to understanding their behavior and provides a basis for curricular and instructional decisions. Rather than adopting elementary or secondary perspectives, developmentally appropriate middle level educators first look to young adolescents' development when making education decisions. They focus attention on planning and implementing a curriculum and a school climate that reflect young adolescents' development.

Chapter 3
Developmentally Appropriate Middle Level Schools

Questions To Be Explored

1. What middle level school curricular and instructional goals reflect young adolescents' physical, psychosocial, and cognitive development?
2. What specific practices can middle level educators implement that reflect current research on the physical, psychosocial, and cognitive development of young adolescents?
3. How can middle level schools help young adolescents deal with contemporary issues related to their development?
4. How can middle level educators evaluate their school's success in addressing students' physical, psychosocial, and cognitive developmental characteristics?
5. How can middle level educators respond to the recommendations in *This We Believe: Developmentally Responsive Middle Level Schools* (National Middle School Association, 1995), *Turning Points* (Carnegie Council on Adolescent Development, 1989), and ACEI's "Child-Centered Middle Schools" position paper (Manning, 2000)?

Except for being a link between the elementary and the secondary schools, the middle level school functioned for too long without a clear rationale. Traditionally considered a transition from the elementary school to the secondary school, the middle level school now is being recognized as a school with a more defined and specific purpose, mainly that of providing young adolescents or 10- to 15-year-olds with developmentally appropriate educational experiences. To accomplish this goal, middle level educators have the twofold responsibility of understanding the early adolescence developmental period and making a commitment to provide young adolescents with opportunities to try out their new physical, psychosocial, and cognitive abilities. This chapter considers ways middle school educators can provide such developmentally appropriate learning experiences.

Meeting Young Adolescents' Developmental Needs

Development during the 10 to 15 age span is characterized by rapid, dramatic, and often disturbing changes. Physical changes occur almost daily, psychosocial changes result in increased social contact and a quest for independence and freedom, and cognitive changes allow higher levels of abstract thinking. While these changes are easily recognized, other more subtle changes also occur. Young adolescents experience increased peer pressure to experiment with tobacco, sex, alcohol, and illegal drugs. Peer pressure, questions about development, and quests for increased freedom have a significant impact on young adolescents, sometimes resulting in greater problems as their development continues. Problems may include experimentation with sexual activity, often leading to sexually transmitted diseases and early pregnancy; use of cigarettes and/or marijuana and other illicit drugs; lower school grades and dropping out; and delinquency and criminal offenses. The early adolescence years may be the best time to provide intervention strategies that help youngsters avoid academic failure and behavior problems. Effective middle level educators address problems resulting from peer pressure, and they value students as individuals. They provide developmentally appropriate educational experiences that reflect a careful balance between academic goals and human development needs. Addressing both academic and developmental needs makes the middle level school program distinctly different from either elementary or secondary programs.

The Developmentally Appropriate Approach

Prior to implementing developmentally appropriate educational practices, schools should select clear priorities that provide a developmental basis for educational practice. Although each school has a responsibility to develop its own priorities, examples may include addressing personal responsibility, building a sense of community, emphasizing academic achievement, and respecting diversity. Upon reaching consensus on these basic priorities, educators then need to plan curricular content, organizational practices, instructional strategies, and a school environment that reflect a commitment to the priorities that contribute to developmentally appropriate practices.

One urban middle school had a number of problems that the faculty thought should be addressed. Students were rowdy and disrespectful, discipline referrals and suspensions were up, and a negative atmosphere prevailed. In essence, the school's priorities included using punishment and negative discipline sanctions to maintain control. The school committee met to determine priorities in light of the problems and decided the school should refocus its priorities to instill a more positive school environment—one that emphasized young adolescents' needs for a positive environment, a sense of community, healthy socialization, and opportunities to learn self-discipline.

Once educators decide on their priorities, middle level education efforts need to include: 1) commonly accepted genuine middle level education philosophical beliefs; 2) a commitment to address young adolescents' developmental characteristics and needs as well as contemporary issues related to their development; and 3) concerted efforts toward the various curricular, organizational, instructional, and environmental aspects, rather than focusing on one entity and retaining traditional elementary or secondary perspectives for others.

Physical Development

Broad curricular and instructional goals related to the young adolescent's physical development include:

- Development of the physical skills necessary to master their bodies
- Adjustment to the hormonal changes that lead to the onset of puberty and development of secondary sex characteristics
- Development of positive attitudes toward nutrition, health, and fitness
- Development of positive attitudes toward tobacco, alcohol, and other drugs.

Appropriate Middle Level School Practices

Seeking a place among their peers, young adolescents realize that their physical abilities have a dramatic influence on their social acceptance and self-perceptions. Middle level schools can provide opportunities for team play and the practice of physical skills so that everyone will have a chance for participation and recognition. Avoiding competition during these physical activities is especially helpful for late-developing young adolescents.

Experiences need to focus on activities such as the 600-yard walk/run; 50-yard dash; skills basic to softball, basketball, volleyball, and soccer; various bowling skills; high and broad jumps; gymnastic stunts (hand stand, hand spring, dive and forward roll, walk on hands, 3-man ride roll); and various types of exercises. Health and physical education activities should reflect the developmental needs of middle level students, rather than being elementary- or secondary-oriented. They also should reflect educators' understanding of young adolescents' tremendous physical diversity.

Topics generally covered in middle level school health education programs generally include sexuality, AIDS and other sexually transmitted diseases, violence prevention, nutrition, emotional wellness, and substance use. These are multifaceted topics with strong affective and behavioral components. Beyond providing factual information, teachers should allow students ample opportunity to reflect on their personal views and how these views affect subsequent behaviors (MacLaury, 2000).

The tremendous physical diversity among young adolescents warrants de-emphasizing activities that stress size, strength, and stamina; recognizing young adolescents' need for physical exercise and their inability to sit still for long periods of time; and providing school policies and behavior expectations that reflect a need for physical activity. One 8th-grade boy, obviously smaller and less mature than the other boys, questioned his development and eventually his self-worth when he could not hit a softball as well as other boys. A few kind words from his physical education teacher had a significant effect during particularly difficult times. The teacher realized that the problem resulted from grouping early- and late-developing students together and forcing them to compete.

With their growing muscles and bones, and often disproportionate bodies, boys and girls become uncomfortable when sitting at desks for long periods of time. One 6th-grade boy who made frequent trips to the pencil sharpener and trash can admitted that he had difficulty sitting comfortably for long periods of time. Perceptive middle level educators provide breaks and exercise periods, as well as learning activities that do not require students to sit (e.g., building projects).

Three Guidelines for Planning Appropriate Physical Experiences

Physical education programs emphasize motor skills and movement, and provide an opportunity to facilitate development in these areas. A developmentally based physical education program can enhance physical fitness and promote a healthful lifestyle and a positive self-image. Several guidelines can help educators plan teaching-learning experiences that reflect 10- to 15-year-olds' physical development. These guidelines hold true whether planning classroom instruction and specific physical education activities or just trying to implement a middle level school program:

- Consider the wide range of developmental diversity among young adolescents when planning programs. Tremendous differences in height, weight, and overall maturity might exist in two boys or girls of the same chronological age. Saying "She's an 11-year-old" conveys little in terms of a physical description.
- Recognize the realities of physical development and their effects on developing self-esteems and identities. Being too short, too tall, overweight, or unduly awkward can have a devastating effect on one's self-perception. One extremely thin 7th-grader suffered almost unbearably. When warm weather came, he continued to wear long-sleeve shirts to prevent others from laughing at his arms. Being the smallest and skinniest in the class affected his self-esteem. He did not participate in sports, even ones that did not require inordinate physical strength, for fear of failure.
- Understand the dangers of competition, recognizing the possible adverse effects when developmentally different learners compete with one another. In terms of strength, size, and speed, the early maturer has a definite advantage over the late-maturing youngster. Avoiding competition does not mean that boys and girls cannot be encouraged to participate with learners of similar development; however, neither embarrassment nor fear of failure should accompany participation in youth sports. In fact, all young adolescents need active engagement in some type of physical activity.

Instructional objectives for programs should include: 1) teaching fundamental physical skills; 2) developing self-esteem, confidence, and loyalty; and 3) developing an appreciation for a healthful lifestyle. In programs that provide positive experiences for 10- to 15-year-olds, educators:

- Encourage participation and interaction in a number of sports and learning physical skills that transfer from sport to sport (Mohnsen & Mendon, 1999)
- Understand and accept that young adolescents are neither elementary nor secondary students
- Understand and accept young adolescents' diversity and skills
- Teach and encourage physical exercise and its importance to physical and psychological well-being
- Acknowledge sportsmanship and team-oriented play
- Talk with students about sports they enjoy

- Emphasize participation, rather than winning
- Teach students that learning physical skills usually includes making mistakes.

Three points about young adolescents and their health concerns deserve mentioning. First, students who are fully engaged in the learning process are usually healthy, while those in poor health tend to have more trouble learning. Second, more than 10 million American children are currently at risk of school failure because of physical, emotional, and social problems. Students who do not feel as though they belong in school are at greater risk of substance abuse, unprotected sex, and violence. Third, the transition from elementary school to middle school can provoke negative academic, social, and psychological consequences for many students. Middle level school educators should take deliberate steps to address all three conditions and behaviors (MacLaury, 2000).

Co-curricular and Intramural Sports Programs

Co-curricular and intramural sports programs should be ones that young adolescents enjoy and that promote participation, interaction, and service. Open to all middle level grade students, these activities can include classroom guidance programs, cheerleading teams, pep squads, and physical activities emphasizing health and physical fitness.

Like all middle level school programs, co-curricular and intramural sports programs should include young adolescents of all maturity levels. Encouraging all students to participate and ensuring that they feel comfortable exhibiting varying degrees of competence provides for improved physical skills and enhanced self-perceptions. Continual professional supervision ensures all students learn correct skills and also prevents students from being forced to compete physically in uncomfortable situations.

Students must not be excluded from interscholastic sports or any intramural team. Rather than denying interested students access, schools can add additional teams. One principal explained how her middle level school planned for four volleyball teams, yet student interest in participation resulted in 10 teams. According to one excited girl who had visited the school, "They have intramural cheerleading teams. No one has to try out—everyone gets to be on a team." Her excitement demonstrates the importance of avoiding competitive and exclusionary policies.

A successful intramural program may be found at Challenger Middle School in Colorado Springs, Colorado. The core of Challenger's program includes providing young adolescents with an opportunity to learn and develop skills. The 6th-grade program is conducted two days a week during the first period. The 7th- and 8th-grade program meets after school. Both programs operate on a player/coach ratio of at least 25 to 1 in all sports. Two unique concepts, cluster coaching and scramble, contribute to the program's effectiveness.

Cluster coaching involves dividing students into two groups or clusters. A cluster then is divided into five balanced teams and either cluster coach can direct the team on a given day. Advantages include: coaches know the caliber of each individual player on the floor at any time; coaches work with 50 or 60 participants, rather than the usual 10 to 15; students benefit from the expertise of two coaches; coaches experience collegial support; and schedules allow for ample evaluation, practice, and competition.

The number of participants in the school's volleyball program grew tremendously; however, nearly half the players failed to complete the season. An informal survey revealed that students felt frustrated with the expertise of some coaches. The same teams always won, while the others lost. Players felt that the coaches' level of knowledge and expertise was a factor.

Challenger began to scramble coaches. The first part of each practice session focuses on teaching and practicing a specific skill. The coach most skilled in that specific area conducts this session. When the lesson is concluded, all the coaches "scramble" to one of the four volleyball nets. Then, the players scramble to one of the eight playing courts. Rather than playing on assigned teams, players are scrambled as long as each team has an equal number. All coaches demonstrate techniques, reinforce efforts, and encourage players (Cicatelli & Gaddie, 1992).

Addressing Young Adolescents' Concerns and Questions About Physical Development

Middle level schools have a responsibility to teach young adolescents about their physical changes: growing arms and legs, hair growth, deepening voices, and the abundance of other changes. In an effort to teach young adolescents about themselves, educators in one suburban middle school focused their attention in several directions. First, they emphasized the normalcy of diversity in developmental and growth rates. Second, they provided factual explanations to young adolescents who questioned their pubertal changes. Realizing that these educational experiences might lead to even greater problems and insecurities, teachers answered questions with accuracy and positive perceptions, countering myths and other false beliefs. Their actual instructional approaches included explanations, factual and age-appropriate publications, adviser-advisee sessions, mini-courses, exploratory offerings, and referrals to the school nurse or guidance counselor.

Addressing Contemporary Issues

Closely related to physical development, health-related issues increasingly pose a concern for 10- to 15-year-olds. Several concerns surface as essential to address in developmentally appropriate practice.

Physical Diversity. Young adolescents' tremendous physical diversity can affect self-esteem and can result in worry about when growth will begin or end. Middle level school educators can play productive roles when they teach young adolescents (perhaps through adviser-advisee programs or exploratory programs) that while all students will experience the same sequence of development, their rate will vary significantly. Early developers sometimes feel more "grown-up" and engage in adult-like behaviors, often participating in activities that have potentially dangerous consequences. Females might feel self-conscious due to their faster growth. Middle school educators need to understand gender differences in physical development and recognize how these differences might affect females' psychosocial development.

Restlessness and Fatigue. Young adolescents often experience restlessness and fatigue due to growing bones, joints, and muscles. They might find sitting for long periods of time more difficult and perhaps even painful when forced to sit at small desks. Exercise should be developmentally appropriate, and physical competition between early- and late-maturing students should be avoided. One perceptive middle school teacher with a significant number of large, early-maturing boys in her class arranged for them to have larger desks. She also gave her class a minute or two to stretch during the middle of extended lessons.

Puberty, Sexual Awareness, and Sexual Identity. Young adolescents' attainment of puberty sometimes results in a sense of sexual awareness that can have dangerous consequences if sexual experimentation occurs. Developmentally appropriate topics can be discussed in health and family life classes, as well as during adviser-advisee programs and exploratory programs.

While all young adolescents face biological and social developmental changes, gay or lesbian young adolescents often struggle with an identity formation that differs from that of the majority of their peers. Estimates suggest there are 2.9 million gay and lesbian students in U.S. schools (Bailey & Phariss, 1996). As they develop their sexual identity, they "feel different" (Taylor, 2000, p. 221) and experience feelings of cognitive dissonance and identity confusion (Taylor, 2000). Some believe that being gay or lesbian and a young adolescent results in double jeopardy. Not only are some of these students fearful, withdrawn, depressed, and full of despair, they often also experience harassment and violence and even may exhibit suicidal tendencies (Vare & Norton, 1998). Others resort to substance abuse, suffer from low self-esteem, and develop conflicts with family members (Bailey & Phariss, 1996).

At-Risk Conditions and Factors. Young adolescents' physical development can be affected by their general health and diet; use of alcohol, drugs, and tobacco; and sexual experimentation that might result in AIDS, STDs, or pregnancy. Eighty-two 5- to 12-year-olds and three hundred twelve 13- to 19-year-olds had AIDS in 1999 (U.S. Bureau of the Census, 2000). Unfortunately, inexperience, a feeling of invincibility, and a lack of knowledge make young adolescents particularly vulnerable. One in four of new HIV infections in the United States occurs in people younger than 22. Since the 20-29 age group accounts for one in five AIDS cases, and the incubation period between HIV infection and AIDS diagnosis is many years, it is possible that large numbers of people diagnosed with HIV and AIDS in their twenties became infected as teenagers (Manning & Bucher, 2001). Middle level school and health and guidance programs are challenged to provide young adolescents with valid information about the circumstances and consequences of the AIDS virus.

Comprehensive school health programs foster healthful lifestyles, coordinate supportive efforts of all school personnel, and provide health-promoting environments. Deliberate responses include individual and group guidance sessions, peer advisement, and counseling programs. Students can be trained to counsel peers, or the counseling team can be called upon for individual or group sessions. Sessions might focus on sex education, developing positive same-sex/other-sex friendships, and understanding self and others. A survey of student concerns might be the most logical place to begin.

The school can set an example by providing a health-promoting environment. Believing that they should practice what they teach about nutrition and healthful choices, administrators at one middle school decided to offer only healthful foods at lunch, providing students with a choice of a healthful, well-balanced meal or a number of fruits and salads.

In schools providing developmentally appropriate experiences, school health coordinators or nurses work closely with middle level school administrators, faculty, and support staff. They coordinate interaction with community health and social service organizations and also design and promote health-related school policies. The classroom teacher, perhaps the first to recognize potential problems related to physical development, works cooperatively with administrators, guidance counselors, the school health coordinator, and other support staff provided by the school or district.

Assessing Middle Level Schools' Response to Young Adolescents' Physical Development

As with all school efforts, educators have a responsibility to assess periodically their progress toward meeting young adolescents' physical needs. Each school needs to develop a suggested checklist to meet its students' individual needs. Appendix A provides a suggested checklist for determining the extent to which a school provides developmentally appropriate experiences.

Psychosocial Development

Broad curricular and instructional goals related to the young adolescent's psychosocial development include development of:

- Competence in personal growth (self-esteem and self-knowledge)
- Positive relationships with peers and adults
- Positive attitudes toward individuals who are culturally diverse
- Positive citizenship skills for living in a democratic society
- Self-discipline, self-exploration, self-direction, and self-responsibility
- Abilities for successful social interaction and friendships
- Skills to become cooperating and contributing members of society.

Appropriate Middle Level School Practices

To be effective, middle level educators need to understand young adolescents' psychosocial development. Psychosocial changes that occur in early adolescence include a quest for independence at a time when youngsters continue to be dependent, a strong desire for peer approval, unusual and drastic behavior, changes in friendships from same-sex to opposite-sex, a preoccupation with one's appearance and mannerisms, and a self-esteem that may fluctuate daily (Manning & Bucher, 2001).

Some educators feel responsible only for cognitive development and academic achievement. They need to recognize, however, that they have a role in assisting young adolescents with their social growth. This role includes not only understanding their psychosocial development, but also providing them opportunities for positive social interaction.

Learners need age- and developmentally appropriate parties and other social get-togethers, rather than "watered-down" versions of secondary dances or activities. Individual physical appearance and ability to purchase expensive clothes should not become significant issues. Young adolescents need opportunities to develop their social skills, rather than yet more times to question their self-worth, developmental levels, economic status, or ability to compete socially.

Socialization opportunities can be developed within the classroom. One middle level school enables interaction through cooperative learning activities (students working in groups of three or four or in pairs), role-playing, writing and putting on plays or skits, allowing friends to work together, teaching social skills, and encouraging membership in clubs.

Responsive middle level educators base education decisions on characteristics unique to the early adolescence developmental period: the need for social interactions and friendships, shifting allegiances and affiliations, peers becoming sources of standards and models of behavior, feelings of anonymity, the need for autonomy and social competence, and developing sex role and special socialization needs (Manning & Bucher, 2001). Other special needs include disabling conditions, mobility and homelessness, and feelings of friendlessness and rejection.

Curricular, Instructional, and Organizational Strategies

Responsive middle level schools promote social development by helping young adolescents develop or enhance friendships, thus making then feel less anonymous. Likewise, they assume social development to include a number of characteristics: self-discipline, perseverance, ability to set and work toward goals, respect for self and others, enthusiasm and interest in learning, confidence, ability to function in a peer group, empathy, trust, communication skills, and awareness of social issues.

Perceptive educators consider the effects of organizational strategies on young adolescents' social development. A fully departmentalized, ability-grouped, seven-period day is incompatible with young adolescents' developmental needs. More appropriate organizational strategies include block-scheduling, multi-age grouping, and other forms of flexible scheduling. In one situation, teachers and the assistant principal met periodically with a consultant for almost one year to discuss the problems with their seven-period day and the possibility of implementing a block schedule. Only after considerable deliberation did the faculty vote to implement a more flexible schedule. The schedule they adopted was sufficiently flexible to accommodate students who preferred to work alone, as well as those who preferred to work in a group. Some students chose to work with a friend to complete a library project; others chose more teacher supervision. In addition to organizational patterns, consideration should be directed toward 10- to 15-year-olds' physical, psychosocial, and cognitive developmental characteristics.

Ability Grouping and Psychosocial Development. Grouping students by ability often results in a form of segregation that can have detrimental effects on self-esteem, socialization, multicultural interaction, and developing identity. Research suggests that low-ability children's attitudes and self-esteem may be seriously impaired by ability grouping. The Carnegie Council on Adolescent Development (1989) contended, "Time and time again, young people are placed in lower academic tracks or classes, often during the middle level grades, [and] are locked into dull, repetitive instructional programs leading at best to minimum competencies" (pp. 50-51).

Ability grouping can adversely affect the attitudes, achievement, and opportunities of students in lower ability groups; segregate students by socioeconomic status and cultural backgrounds; and decrease self-esteem among students in the lower ability groups. For example, self-esteem tends to peak during the early elementary years and decline in the middle level years (Manning & Bucher, 2001). For young adolescents in lower ability groups, self-esteem becomes increasingly negative as each year passes. These youngsters, who judge themselves constantly, can develop distorted views of themselves in lower ability groups segregated by racial or ethnic lines.

Educators concerned about the negative effects of ability grouping can turn to several alternatives: heterogeneous grouping, multiage grouping (Elmore & Wisenbaker, 2000; Hopping, 2000; Moss & Fuller, 2000), individualized instruction, and cooperative learning. In these heterogeneous arrangements, learners interact with students of other ability levels and ethnic backgrounds. The most effective strategies avoid group labels, provide quality and equitable instructional quality, reassess students and group assignments, and counterbalance ability groups with social or academic activities that encourage interaction among peers of different abilities and backgrounds.

School-Within-a-School (SWS). Even when educators carefully project future school growth and population changes, schools often grow so large that students experience feelings of anonymity. To avoid such feelings among young adolescents, middle level schools should include:

- Small, secure, and comfortable organizational sections in which learners feel known by other students and by at least one adult
- Physical separation by grade level within the building
- A focus on belonging and identity for both young adolescents and teachers
- A structure that allows teachers and students to plan and work collaboratively in learning situations.

The School-Within-a-School (SWS), one means of achieving such an organizational approach, organizes students into separate "schools" or "houses" using chronological age-grade grouping that represents the overall demographics of the larger school. In such schools, teachers become familiar with their colleagues and may confer with others frequently about the progress of students. The Carnegie Council on Adolescent Development (1989) suggested the SWS approach as a solution to large schools. A "house" may contain 200 to 300 students, but no more than 500.

> Students in the house would constitute a microcosm of the school population in ethnic and socioeconomic backgrounds and in physical, emotional, and cognitive maturity, allowing students to learn from each other about human diversity. Students should remain in the same house as long as they were enrolled in the school, and view themselves as graduates of the house as well as of the school. (p. 38)

One middle level school with an enrollment of 1,000 students elected to divide into two separate campuses of approximately 500 students, each with its own administrative body. Then, four units of approximately 125 students each provided a further defined sense of identity. The two schools continued to exist in one building. Students from one school, however, did not interact with students from the other during any time of the day. Students felt better about their school and teachers and had more opportunities for socialization.

Another "School-Within-a-School," at Irmo Middle School in Columbia, South Carolina, encouraged young adolescents to feel a sense of belonging and commitment to the school. "Spirit Week" featured developmentally appropriate activities designed to make students more aware of other young adolescents, as well as the institution itself. Wearing school colors, students participated in contests (designed to ensure that winning did not depend on developmental levels!) and group performances. Parents and families were invited to the school on Friday nights to enjoy the school spirit and learn more about the school's efforts. Throughout the week, efforts focused on making students feel a significant part of the school.

Classroom Environment. The classroom environment plays a major role in the success of teaching-learning efforts and promoting positive psychosocial development. The ACEI position paper on "Child-Centered Middle Schools" calls for a "positive and safe learning environment that emphasizes cooperation, collaboration, and peaceful existence, and that is physically and psychologically safe and free from all teasing, bullying, and harassment—in other words, an environment that shows care and concern" (ACEI/Manning, 2000, p. 154).

Kohn (1996a) believes that educators must provide for three universal human needs if they are to provide positive learning environments: autonomy, relatedness, and competence. Students who are autonomous have self-determination or the ability to make decisions, rather than being at the mercy of events outside of their control. When they are related, students have a connection to others and a sense of affirmation and belonging. Finally, students have an inherent desire to be competent, learn new things, acquire skills, and put them to use.

Kohn (1996a) believed that "schools will not become inviting, productive places for learning until we have dispensed with bribes and threats altogether" (p. 36). Making students suffer in order to alter their future behavior may result in temporary compliance, but this approach probably will not help students become ethical or compassionate decision-makers. Rather than promoting reason, punishment damages relationships between teachers and students, and tends to generate anger, defiance, and a desire for revenge.

One 6th-grade teacher worked purposely to build a positive, learner-centered classroom in which students were managed without threats, bribes, or punishments. She faced a difficult task because her students had been conditioned during their previous school experiences to equate school with coercion, control, and punishments. Working to change their mindset about what school could be like, she worked daily to promote teacher-student and student-student collaboration, encourage students to make decisions that affected them and their learning, and align curricular experiences with developmental needs. She believed the advantages of the resulting positive classroom environment (e.g., one that reflected the middle level school concept) would be worth her efforts.

Kohn links his focus on learning and the classroom environment to an emphasis on positive behaviors, and believes in learner-centered classrooms in which the climate or environment is "often guided by a certain set of values, a vision of what school *ought* (Kohn's italics) to be like" (Kohn, 1996b, p. 54). In these rooms, teachers work collaboratively with students, encourage students to make decisions, and use student interests and questions to drive much of the curriculum. Promoting deep understanding, teachers should build on students' natural curiosity and desire to become competent, and should help students become proficient learners (Kohn, 1997).

Payne, Conroy, and Racine (1998) maintain that the "right" (p. 65) atmosphere or environment in a school can make or break the entire school program. A positive school climate contributes to student achievement, empowers teachers and students to take risks, fosters critical thinking and problem-solving, and helps students take pride in their school efforts.

A positive school climate also involves students, staff, parents, and the community in a partnership. Young adolescents need to see themselves as valued members of a group that offers supportive and trusting relationships. They need to feel successful and to be praised and rewarded for that success. They need to become socially competent individuals who have the skills necessary to cope with everyday life. They need to believe they have a promising future and have the competence and motivation to take advantage of the opportunities society has to offer (Carnegie Council on Adolescent Development, 1989).

A positive classroom environment is characterized by the following:

- The environment promotes creativity, responsible risk-taking, cooperation, and mutual trust and respect
- Staff and students feel safe in classes and all school-related activities

- Staff, students, and parents find the learning environment to be academically stimulating
- Community involvement in the school (by parents, volunteers, and community business partners)
- High daily attendance
- Positive attitudes of teachers, students, and parents
- A sense of ownership and pride in one's school
- High rates of participation in schoolwide and systemwide activities
- Positive media coverage
- Rigorous academic expectations for all students. (Payne, Conroy, & Racine, 1998)

A positive school environment also includes a positive verbal environment—one that enhances learners' self-esteem and the overall quality of the school experience. Unlike negative environments that cause children to feel unworthy, incompetent, or insignificant, positive verbal environments satisfy children's psychological needs and make them feel valued. In positive verbal environments, educators:

- Use words to show genuine interest in young adolescents, their lives, and their interests
- Send positive and accepting verbal and nonverbal messages
- Listen attentively to what young adolescents have to say
- Speak politely to children
- Use classroom conversations as a basis for opportunities to involve all young adolescents in classroom communication
- Avoid judgmental comments about children, either to them directly or within their hearing.

A positive school environment also includes a commitment to civility. Plucker (2000) maintained that a significant problem facing contemporary schools is incivility. Emotional and verbal violence can be just as damaging as physical violence, although its effects might not be as visible. In fact, lack of respect and constructive communication forms the foundation of incivility and should be treated assertively. For this to occur, students need to feel they belong, to have opportunities to make real choices, to realize communication is the key hurdle to preventing violence, and to know the consequences of their actions (Plucker, 2000).

In summary, young adolescents deserve learning environments that contribute to feelings of success, recognition, and respect. These positive classroom environments provide opportunities for young adolescents to achieve academically and develop social competence in safe and secure school environments.

Cooperative Learning—Psychosocial Benefits. Students who work in teams learn to interact successfully with others. Research suggests that social skills improve when learners work cooperatively toward a particular goal, and that some learners may need direct instruction in social skills if they are to participate effectively in cooperative situations. Students express greater liking for peers in cooperative learning groups. Relationships improve as students engage in positive interdependence, face-to-face interaction, individual accountability, and social skills. For cooperative learning to be effective, students must get to know one another, communicate accurately and unambiguously, accept and support one another, and resolve conflicts constructively (Slavin, 1996).

Cross-cultural Grouping. When allowed to choose group members, students usually select same-sex members of similar cultural or socioeconomic backgrounds. In cross-cultural grouping, teachers organize students in groups that are diverse in gender, culture, ethnicity, and social class. Research on such cooperative learning indicates that students who work and study together form more positive feelings about one another.

Teacher-Student Teams. Teaming provides opportunities for groups to work together toward academic and personal goals and to solve problems before they reach a crisis stage. This community of learners nurtures bonds between teachers and students and serves as a key building block in young adolescents' education. Teaming also provides an environment conducive to learning by reducing feelings of anonymity and isolation. Schools with successful teams have sufficient staff to make teams as small as possible, so teams know each other well (Carnegie Council on Adolescent Development, 1989).

Adviser-Advisee Program. Three significant works, *This We Believe* (National Middle School Association, 1995), *Turning Points* (Carnegie Council on Adolescent Development, 1989), and *Turning Points 2000* (Jackson & Davis, 2000), documented the need for middle level school educators to address affective as well as cognitive concerns. Young adolescents need guidance and support as they struggle to cope with the changing world and their changing selves. *This We Believe* called for middle level schools to provide a caring adult to give young adolescents the individual attention they deserve. In fact, *This We Believe* identified advisory programs as one of the 10 essential components of effective middle school design (Brown, 2001). Similarly, *Turning Points* suggested that every middle level school student should be well-known by at least one adult. The adviser-advisee program serves this function. Last, *Turning Points 2000* (Jackson & Davis, 2000) advocates for advisory programs, maintaining that "when students make lasting connections with at least one caring adult, academic and personal outcomes improve" (p. 143).

The primary purpose of advisory programs is to provide the time and environment for developing significant relationships between each student and teacher-adviser (Brown, 2001). Sometimes referred to as teacher-based guidance, the adviser-advisee program ensures that all students have at least one adult who knows them well, and also that all students belong to a small interactive group. Advisory groups seek to promote students' social, emotional, and moral growth while providing personal and academic guidance. To reduce the student-teacher ratio, all faculty serve as advisers, including exploratory teachers, librarians, and resource teachers. The most successful sessions occur at the beginning of each day and last at least 30 minutes.

Advisers serve advisees as friend, advocate, guide, group leader, community builder, liaison with parents, and evaluation coordinator. They also provide a warm, caring environment, plan and implement advisory programs, assist advisees in monitoring academic progress, provide times for students to share concerns, refer advisees to appropriate resources, communicate with parents and families, maintain appropriate records, and encourage advisees' cognitive and psychosocial growth. Activities during adviser-advisee sessions include meeting with individual students about problems; offering various guidance activities; discussing academic, personal, and family problems; addressing ethical issues; discussing multicultural issues and relations; and helping students with esteem and confidence problems. Teacher-advisers should know each young adolescent as an individual; develop a secure and comfortable classroom atmosphere; try self-disclosure to show that teachers also have problems, satisfactions, and challenges; and show concern for a student's problem or worry. The adviser-advisee program also provides an excellent opportunity to discuss the many questions and concerns young adolescents have about their development (Manning & Bucher, 2001).

Effective advisory sessions require careful planning. Advisory plans need to have written objectives; advisory-related problems and issues can be discussed in faculty meetings. Also, effective advisories require clearly established ground rules, such as that comments offered during advisories are confidential; differences are respected; problems at home or with other teachers can be shared (the teacher's name cannot be mentioned); and problems involving abuse, crime, and drugs should not be discussed except individually with the teacher.

Wantagh Middle School in Wantagh, New York, started an advisory program with volunteers who believed that young adolescents need individual adult attention. The program includes almost every member of the staff: teachers, administrators, librarians, and guidance counselors. Wantagh seeks to provide an adult advocate for each young adolescent. This adult sees the advisee in the morning, monitors student progress, and serves as the first line of communication between home and school. Now in its fifth year, the program has an advisory handbook and extended advisories that are held twice monthly. Some advisory sessions have a set purpose, while others are left to the adviser's discretion. Benefits include the opportunity to know students in a nonacademic setting and to work with all ability groups. Also, staff and special area teachers become a part of the total school program (Andrews & Stern, 1992).

Brown (2001) described an advisory at Tilden Middle School in Philadelphia, Pennsylvania, an urban middle school with a student population that is 90 percent African American. All students at Tilden qualify for free lunch. The teachers at Tilden attended a one-week session to learn how to implement an effective advisory program. Advisory sessions at Tilden are held once a week for 50 minutes at the beginning of the school day. Teachers work to prioritize student goal setting; address students' concerns about sexual issues; respond to students' drug and alcohol concerns; identify students' needs for caring relationships; recognize other stress factors, such as urban students needing a child-like environment; address conflicts among students; and address safety concerns (Brown, 2001).

Peer Advising. Young adolescents can play significant advisory roles as they help peers through psychosocial changes. Educators working with young adolescents can attest to the tremendous influence of peer pressure. While peer pressure often has a negative connotation, perceptive educators take advantage of it by channeling positive suggestions and constructive advice to students. Young adolescents may feel more comfortable confiding in peers than in a teacher, guidance counselor, or other adult. To become a reality, a peer advising program needs only minimal training of students. Peer advisers can refer pupils to the counselor, if needed.

Improving Self-Esteem. Educators long have recognized how a sense of self-worth affects one's social development, as well as her or his motivation and academic achievement. While positive self-esteem is important for students at all grade levels, middle school educators have an extra responsibility because self-esteem often declines, especially for girls, during the middle school years. Changing from elementary school to middle school, developing bodies, making new friends and sometimes losing older friends, and taking on more difficult subject matter can negatively affect self-esteems. Middle school educators face a twofold challenge: first, they need to teach young adolescents to make accurate assessments of their self-esteem and, second, they need to provide educational experiences that contribute to positive self-esteem (Manning & Bucher, 2001).

Responsive middle level educators provide educational experiences designed to improve young adolescents' self-esteem. Teachers, administrators, and other professionals need to:

- Know young adolescents, their developmental needs, and their thinking abilities
- Speak to students by name in classrooms and halls, ask about activities, and acknowledge personal achievements
- Allow small groups of students to work together on productive activities, both for academic and social learning
- Convey to students a sense of belief in their ability to learn, succeed, and behave
- Recognize young adolescents' developmental needs and characteristics
- Offer learning experiences that address friendship and other socialization issues affecting young adolescents
- Offer young adolescents meaningful roles in learning activities (e.g., involving them in planning and evaluating learning experiences).

Opportunities To Participate in Developmentally Appropriate Social Functions. Students need developmentally appropriate opportunities to mingle socially and improve their social skills, not "watered-down" versions of secondary experiences. Activities should not focus primarily on boy-girl pairing. During early adolescence, same-sex friendships take precedence; as development continues, cross-sex friendships will begin to develop.

At one 6th-grade social function, the boys stood on one side of the room and threw popcorn at the girls. The girls stood on the other side and mostly giggled. A degree of social interaction was occurring: the boys acknowledged the girls by throwing popcorn and the girls acknowledged their actions by giggling. While some adults might perceive this situation as "silly" or a "waste of time," this social interaction represented a beginning. Later that evening, some of the girls and boys talked to each other. During social occasions later in the semester, more cross-over occurred among the groups. The teachers understood the nature of young adolescent friendships and did not try to force cross-over among the groups. At no time did they force social interaction or chastise the boys and girls for their behavior.

Rather than isolating or segregating young adolescents who like to socialize, some middle level educators recognize young adolescents' need for social interaction, and so provide opportunities for friends to be together throughout the school day. These educators actually encourage social interaction by placing students with friends in the cafeteria, in their units and classes, and during break periods. Other socialization opportunities include academic honors clubs, special interest clubs, debate teams, and committees. Socialization can also occur in learning groups.

Addressing Young Adolescent Concerns and Questions About Psychosocial Development. Young adolescents who understand the process of their psychosocial-emotional development become less preoccupied with personal matters and thus are better prepared to cope with a rapidly changing society. Helping young adolescents better understand themselves can take several directions:

- Middle level educators can help learners understand their shifting emphasis from a parent-centered world to a peer-centered world. Rather than feeling guilty or disobedient, the learner understands that such behavior is normal.
- Young adolescents need to be aware that friendships and cliques change. A student shunned by a clique one day might be readily accepted another day. Educators can help young adolescents understand the changing nature of friendships.
- Although caring middle level educators strive to make all students feel accepted by the school and the various peer groups, some young adolescents still feel a sense of anonymity. The move from elementary school to middle level school and the transitory nature of friendships and cliques can result in students feeling "lost."
- Young adolescents need to realize that while resisting peer pressure can damage friendships, adhering to one's personal beliefs is more important.

Even in the midst of an already overcrowded day, middle level schools can provide academic and socialization sessions that help young adolescents understand themselves. Effective approaches may include opportunities for social interaction, appropriate large- or small-group classroom activities, adviser-advisee sessions, minicourses, guidance counselors, community speakers, and parent participators.

Addressing Contemporary Issues

As with physical development, certain contemporary issues associated with psychosocial development confront young adolescents. These issues may vary with grade level, geographical region, developmental maturity, and social class. Still, some issues are fairly common throughout early adolescence.

One contemporary issue is the change in parent and family relationships. Elkind (1995) looked at the school and family in what he called the "postmodern world" (p. 8). Young adolescents reside in a variety of family types—two-parent working, single-parent, remarried, and adoptive families—all representative of the changing kinship structures in postmodern America. Elkind notes that while the nuclear family may be the least stressful family type in present-day society, many nuclear families are far from ideal and many non-nuclear families do an excellent job of child rearing (Elkind, 1995).

A second contemporary issue is the urgency many young adolescents feel (perhaps from peer pressure, media images, or even parents) to move quickly into adolescence or early adulthood. Elkind (1995) maintains that adolescents are seen as *sophisticated* (Elkind's italics, p. 13). They are quite knowledgeable about drugs, sex, sexually transmitted diseases, and AIDS (Elkind, 1995). They are undoubtedly influenced by media portrayals of teenagers who are sexually active and may be using drugs, and consider themselves equal to their parents in decision-making competence (Elkind, 1995).

Young adolescents' urge to rush through early adolescence and on into adolescence can take a significant toll, as evidenced in the high incidences of teenage pregnancy and sexually transmitted diseases and stress-related ailments. Drug use is prevalent among disturbing numbers of 12- to 17-year-olds. In 1998, drug use among 12- to 17-year-olds included marijuana and hashish at 8.8 percent, cocaine at .08 percent, and alcohol at 19.1 percent (U.S. Bureau of the Census, 2000). Regarding smoking, the good news is that anti-smoking campaigns, the increased cost of cigarettes, and new attitudes about smoking have resulted in a decrease in smoking among 8th-graders. From 1996 to 2001, the percentage of 8th-graders who smoke declined from 21 percent to 12 percent (Fountain, 2001). Considering some students start smoking as early as 11 or 12 years, 12 percent is still a disturbing number—especially considering the addictive nature of tobacco.

Young adolescents sometimes adopt adult behaviors, yet their psychosocial development has not matured sufficiently to deal with substance use, academic pressure, peer-group situations, and relationships with the opposite sex. Such issues have special significance for middle level educators, who all too often see young adolescents being hurried into adolescence and on into adulthood. Middle level schools can help young adolescents deal with these contemporary issues by:

- Treating early adolescence as an important developmental period with its own unique developmental characteristics and life tasks
- Recognizing the importance of contributing not only to learners' academic growth, but also to their self-esteem and social and emotional development
- Providing age-appropriate activities that de-emphasize competition, such as intramural athletics
- Providing social activities that involve all students, rather than only boy-girl activities

- Treating contemporary issues, such as peer pressure and growing up too fast, in adviser-advisee groups, guidance programs, and special curricular areas.

Assessing Middle Level Schools' Response to Psychosocial Development

The "Psychosocial Development" section of the checklist in Appendix A can be used to assess a school's efforts. This checklist serves as a beginning point for a more comprehensive assessment designed especially for one's individual school.

Cognitive Development

Broad curricular and instructional goals related to the young adolescent's cognitive development include:

- Application of basic skills mastered in the elementary grades and the continued learning of basic skills by those learners still needing basic skills instruction
- Understanding of the interrelatedness of subject areas
- Development of higher order thinking and reasoning skills
- Acquisition of ethical and moral thinking abilities
- Development of cognitive skills necessary for lifelong learning
- Exploratory opportunities to provide broad exposure to cognitive activities, in addition to a continuing emphasis on academic subject areas.

Appropriate Middle Level School Practices

What developmentally appropriate practices address the above goals and also reflect contemporary research on cognitive development?

First, with the onset of formal operations, some young adolescents develop an increasing ability to think. This developing ability demands increased opportunities for critical thinking and problem-solving activities. They also can see, for the first time, connections between present achievements and future aspirations. They are better able to conduct a realistic appraisal of their abilities and academic potential. It is important to emphasize, however, that some middle level school learners continue to function at the concrete operations stage. Their maturity does not allow them to work effectively with highly conceptual content or with abstract thought processes such as analogy, hypothesis, and deduction. Instruction for these students should be rich in experience, demonstration, practice, and personal relevance. Developmentally appropriate instruction (or instruction that meets young adolescents' higher or lower cognitive levels) requires evaluating students to determine cognitive levels and careful planning to ensure instruction is appropriate. Second, young adolescents' increasing ability to see relationships and to synthesize information suggests the need for interdisciplinary units of study that cross subject area lines. Third, educators need to provide an intellectually stimulating environment, with opportunities to work collaboratively and engage in exploratory activities.

Developmentally appropriate learning experiences challenge, yet do not over-challenge, students. Over-challenged students are subject to academic failure, frustration, and lower self-esteem. A carefully articulated curriculum also minimizes gaps as students move from unit to unit or grade to grade. Such a curriculum provides a clear articulation between elementary and secondary curricula. Middle level learning activities reflect student variance in levels of reading, thinking, attention span and concentration, and interest. Educators recognize and plan for differences in students' ability to generalize and to understand abstract concepts, as well as differences in interests and goals, cognitive responsiveness, and personal adjustment.

Ability Grouping and Cognitive Development. A previous discussion of grouping and psychosocial development explained how ability grouping can detrimentally affect socialization. Grouping by ability also can have harmful effects on young adolescents' cognitive development.

Several factors suggest ability grouping has a negative impact on students' overall development. First, grouping students by academic ability can have a devastating impact on how teachers think about students and how students think about themselves. Second, contrary to what some educators think, ability grouping does not enhance student achievement and actually may reduce achievement levels among average- and low-ability learners. Third, ability grouping might provide "good" students one curriculum, while the "poor" students receive a watered-down version. Teachers sort out students and relegate them to separate tracks for fast, medium, and slow learners. Fourth, teachers often interact differently with students in the various ability groups. Fifth, grouping by ability may seriously impair the self-esteem of lower ability learners.

Also disturbing, ability grouping patterns often parallel students' nonacademic characteristics, such as race or ethnicity, socioeconomic status, and personal appearance. Learners from lower socioeconomic status and from culturally diverse backgrounds placed in lower ability groups may be victims of discrimination if they are segregated along ethnic and social class lines (Jackson & Davis, 2000).

While ability grouping is fairly common in some schools, middle level school educators—in fact, all educators—should work toward heterogeneous grouping. Such an effort should include high expectations for all students; support from both teachers and parents; careful planning, based on sound research; and adequate staff development in alternatives to homogeneous grouping. Ability grouping should be avoided for both psychosocial and cognitive reasons; when school or district policies mandate ability grouping, however, special attention should be given to assigning students to classes that reflect diversity in gender, ethnicity, social class, and developmental maturity.

The National Middle School Association (1995) took the position that a fully departmentalized, ability-grouped, seven-period day was incompatible with research on young adolescents and their cognitive characteristics. Likewise, all national reports and state studies on middle level school education recommended the elimination of tracking students by academic ability. How, then, can middle level educators avoid the hazards of homogeneous ability grouping? Chart 3.1 looks at several alternatives to this type of grouping.

Many middle level educators group students heterogeneously and then regroup them within the large group. This organizational approach can occur within and across student teams, allowing flexibility in arranging instructional times, resources, space, equipment, and teachers.

Chart 3.1
Alternatives to Homogeneous Ability Grouping

Grouping Method	A Brief Description
Heterogeneous	Students grouped without regard to ability or academic achievement
Developmental Age	Students grouped according to development or maturity levels
Multiage	Students grouped across age levels and according to individual needs and interests
Cooperative Learning	Students grouped in pairs or small groups, working together toward group goals
Regrouping	Students "regrouped" within the heterogeneous group
Cross-age Tutoring	Students grouped whereby older students tutor younger learners, assisting both groups' learning and achievement

---

Developmentally Appropriate Programs: Considerations

Cognitive Readiness Levels. Young adolescents' emerging cognitive capabilities require developmentally appropriate learning strategies and study skills. Such teaching-learning experiences also should reflect an understanding of young adolescents' vast diversity in cognitive development.

Cognitive developmental characteristics of young adolescents include their increasing ability to:

- Begin formal operations and the accompanying intellectual exercises
- Use cognitive skills to solve real-life problems
- Deal with hypotheses involving two or more variables
- Deal with abstract concepts and difficult academic concepts
- Think critically and reflectively, as well as hypothetically

- Argue to convince others and clarify own thinking
- Make generalizations
- Make judgments regarding behavior and develop a sense of morality, ethical behavior, and self-discipline
- Take another's point of view
- Develop personal attitudes and perspectives
- Develop independence and a concern for interdependence
- Develop increasing recognition of cultural and other types of diversity.

Learning How To Learn. Teaching students to "learn how to learn" is a critical goal in the 21st century. A rapidly increasing knowledge base, technological breakthroughs, and students' growing cognitive abilities in the learning process all indicate that learning will increasingly be considered a lifelong process. Young adolescents have developed cognitively to a point where they can now play a greater role in their own learning. Their social development allows cooperative efforts, their cognitive development allows higher levels of thought, and their overall maturity provides a sense of responsibility as they progress toward the goal of independent learning.

Perceptive educators emphasize student responsibility for learning by encouraging students to be active, rather than passive, learners and to be problem-solvers, inquirers, and seekers of information. To reach these goals, they encourage young adolescents to:

- State what they expect to achieve by using a specific skill
- Describe the procedures and rules they plan to use as they employ the skill
- Predict the results of their use of the skill
- Check the procedure they use as they employ the skill
- Evaluate the outcome of using the skill and the way they employed it.

As young adolescents engage in the process of learning how to learn, educators can help them look for new information in readings, presentations, and discussions; identify information that helps explain the relevance of what is already understood; recognize or create patterns and relationships that help break down complex concepts into manageable components; and develop strategies to represent relationships among parts and wholes.

Equal Access to All School Experiences and Programs. All students should have equal opportunity to participate in educational experiences. Instructional practices that hinder students from reaching the most advanced curricular levels and prevent them from achieving at the highest levels mock the concept of equal access. Numerous violations of this equal access concept are found in middle level schools today. For example:

- An 8th-grade girl tried out for cheerleading with over 100 other girls, even though only 15 would be selected. She memorized the cheers, learned the jumps, and gave four days to the pursuit; nevertheless, the girl failed to "make the team." The school failed to provide equal access to over 86 girls, including the girl who practiced diligently to become a member of the team.

- A 7th-grade girl tried out for the school play. She remained after school and faithfully participated in the tryouts. Nearly 100 students tried out for the available parts. This time, however, even worse odds faced female would-be participants: of the 11 parts, the teachers needed only four girls! Not only did the school violate the concept of equal access, but the girls faced even more difficult obstacles.

- Another middle level school required 7th-grade students to choose among art, music, and band. A young learner, showing talent and interest in both art and music, faced a difficult decision because the school schedule did not allow participation in all three areas or even in two areas.

Educators can provide students equal access to all programs and activities. For example:

- One middle school principal assured parents that all students would have an opportunity to participate on cheerleading teams. "We have 10 cheerleading teams. If more girls want to join a team, then we will begin additional teams." The school offered similar commitments for volleyball, soccer, and other sports.

- Another time, teachers announced the opportunity to participate in a play. All students participated: some had speaking roles, others sang as a group. Everyone had the opportunity to be on stage. Other possibilities included having more than one play, or perhaps having a series of one-act plays scheduled over a weekend or even several weekends.

Appropriate Curricular, Instructional, and Organizational Strategies

Core Curriculum. Middle level core curriculum includes specific subject areas (e.g., language arts, mathematics, science, social studies) as well as broader learnings. Both subject matter and instructional methods need to satisfy cognitive, affective, and psychomotor development in a full and balanced program. Broader learnings include thinking critically, solving problems, developing healthful lifestyles, and being active citizens. Using the terminology "core curriculum" should not imply that subject areas should be taught separately or piecemeal. Middle level schools can integrate subject matter across disciplines and provide this core of common knowledge, attitudes, and skills through exploratory programs and interdisciplinary studies (Manning & Bucher, 2001).

Although all young adolescents should have equal access to the middle level core curriculum, actual content and instructional strategies should be developmentally appropriate. For example, some young adolescents might need concrete learning experiences, while others might need more abstract learning experiences. Developmental, gender, and cultural differences, as well as various individual differences, need to be considered as educators reach decisions on specific curricular content.

Integration of Curricular Areas. Some middle level educators feel strongly that the curriculum should be taught through an interdisciplinary, thematic approach (Moss & Fuller, 2000). Through integrated curriculum, the various curricular areas are integrated using topics, themes, and subject areas to promote interdisciplinary learning and to allow students to connect learning from one subject area to another, to real-world situations, and to their own experiences (Manning & Bucher, 2001). Sometimes called problem-based learning, integrated curriculum can be based around problems (e.g., pollution and inequality) that young adolescents' psychosocial and cognitive development allow them to understand.

To acquire and use knowledge productively, middle level students need to understand that knowledge and skills cross subject areas. Yet, school curricula traditionally have been organized as territorial spaces carved out by academic scholars for their own purposes. Such an organization limits access to broader meanings by not allowing learners to cross subject area boundaries when seeking answers to questions.

ACEI has taken a stand in favor of integrated curriculum: "Regardless of the curricular model(s) selected, a middle school curriculum that centers on the child should include interdisciplinary or integrated curricular approaches, so that young adolescents will perceive the relationships among curricular areas" (ACEI/Manning, 2000, p. 156).

Tom Erb (1999) explained that an integrated curriculum focuses on problems, questions, or themes that are investigated for their own inherent interest and significance. These might include such concepts as communities, conflict and compromise, the future, global awareness, wellness, transitions, justice, or identities.

Why is the topic of curriculum integration enjoying such interest and support among middle school educators? The answers may be found in the writing of James A. Beane, one of the most vocal proponents of the integrated curriculum. Beane (1996) identifies several reasons for the attention. First, more educators favor curriculum arrangements that involve application of knowledge over rote memorization. Second, research on brain functions indicates that the brain looks for patterns and connections and emphasizes coherence over fragmentation. By extension, the more that learning and knowledge is unified, the more accessible and "brain-compatible" it is. Third, there is a shift in education from knowing the "right answer" to knowing how to find the best solution. Knowledge is neither fixed nor universal. Today's students are being asked to answer questions and face situations that did not exist when their parents went to school. When solving today's complex problems dealing with the environment, medical ethics, or human relations, students need to apply information from an assortment of disciplines and use a collection of information gathering strategies. Finally, the movement toward an integrated middle school curriculum is being driven by professional educators who are seriously interested in progressive education approaches such as whole language, unit teaching, thematic curriculum, and problem- and project-centered methods (Beane, 1996).

In fact, educators find integrative instruction attractive at the middle level for several reasons. It encourages faculty members to cross previously impenetrable boundaries to school subjects. It seems to make learning more connected and less fragmented for young adolescents. It even appears to offer opportunities to "connect" in the classroom for students with differing readiness levels, interests, and learning profiles (Tomlinson, 1998). Plus, curricular integration helps young adolescents become independent, confident students who develop lifelong learning skills. Young adolescents' cognitive development permits an understanding of the relationships and principles that cross curricular lines.

Chart 3.2 shows some of the contexts of integrated teaching as identified by Beane (1996).

Chart 3.2
Contexts of an Integrated Middle School Curriculum

- Teachers and students collaboratively identify a problem or issue that will serve as the integrating theme
- Ten- to 15-year-olds consider the issue under discussion to be of personal and social significance
- The problem or issue becomes the central focus of the curriculum, rather than an add-on
- Learning experiences relate specifically to the issue and integrate knowledge from as many curricular areas as possible
- Subject lines dissolve as the emphasis is placed on integrative exploration
- Students acquire knowledge and skills to solve the problem or issue being studied rather than merely accumulating facts or skills
- Projects and activities involve the real application of knowledge
- Young adolescents see how this experience can be used in other situations
- Students see the benefits of problem solving.

Based on: Beane, J. (1996). On the shoulders of giants! The case for curriculum integration. *Middle School Journal, 28*(1), 6-11.

For curricular integration to become a reality, two crucial aspects warrant recognition. First, integration implies wholeness and unity, rather than separation and fragmentation. Second, genuine curricular integration occurs when young people confront personally meaningful questions and engage in related experiences they can integrate into their own system of meanings (Beane, 1996).

The insistence on a core academic program sometimes leads educators to believe that subjects should be taught separately. The core curriculum, however, can be organized around integrated themes that young adolescents find relevant to their own lives. For example, English, arts, history, and social studies courses may be grouped into humanities and then organized around thematic units, such as "Immigration." Likewise, mathematics and science may be grouped in themes such as "Mapping the Environment" (Carnegie Council on Adolescent Development, 1989). Other interdisciplinary or thematic units include "Developing Through Early Adolescence," "Making Wise Decisions," "Young Adolescents Around the World," "Technology and People," "Cultural Diversity," "Weather," and "Time."

Interdisciplinary Team Organization. Interdisciplinary team organization (ITO) involves a team of two or more subject teachers who share students and planning time and who work to draw connections among their subjects. While teachers might teach together at times, that is not a requirement for interdisciplinary team teaching (Manning & Bucher, 2001). Unfortunately, interdisciplinary teaming is the exception rather than the rule in some middle level schools. With barely half of the middle level schools in the nation even claiming to engage in interdisciplinary teaming, much work remains to be done to provide young adolescents and their teachers with the tools necessary for quality middle grades education (Erb, 1999). Still, interdisciplinary teaming offers advantages for both young adolescents and teachers and, therefore, should be considered an essential practice in developmentally appropriate middle level schools.

The most common of all middle level school organizations, interdisciplinary teams consist of a group of teachers, usually two to five, who represent different disciplines but share a common group of students, a common schedule and planning time, and an adjacent space whenever possible (Erb, 1997). In an extensive report on a longitudinal study of a school network engaged in *Turning Points*-based school transformation, Felner et al. (1997) offered some interesting findings on the structure of teams. First, they found that team sizes can range from 60-70 students with two-to-three teachers to more than 240 students with nine-to-twelve teachers. Student-to-teacher ratios on a team vary from 20 students per teacher to more than 40 students per teacher. Also, the amount of common planning time varies from no common planning time, to shared use of individual planning times, to daily common planning times provided in addition to individual planning time for every teacher.

The basic rationale for ITO in middle schools is that it provides a more effective means of meeting the developmental needs and individual interests of 10- to 15-year-olds. It minimizes the number of young adolescents who feel unknown, who think that teachers do not know their progress in other classes, or who believe that other students do not know them well enough to accept them as friends. Because of the closer, more coherent supervision and caring that occurs on a team, ITO helps students build team spirit and improves attitudes and work habits. On interdisciplinary teams where teachers share a common planning time, students have higher self-concepts and both students and teachers have more positive feelings about school (Warren & Muth, 1995). Interdisciplinary teams also offer unique opportunities for team members to collaborate on curricular and instructional decisions.

In addition to improving instruction and developing better interpersonal relationships, effective teams can become powerful forces in creating learning communities for both teachers and students (Martin, 1999). Other advantages include an

ITO's contributions to both the school environment and the curriculum. Interdisciplinary team organization is necessary to create a positive school environment that emphasizes caring, respect, success, and interdependence (Felner et al., 1997). From a curricular perspective, interdisciplinary teaming establishes a curricular balance among content, instruction, and skills for general, career, and fine arts education, while also providing students with a better understanding about the interconnectedness of the various content areas. Similarly, planning time, materials, and other resources can be shared by professionals.

What are some benchmarks of effective interdisciplinary teams? Here are a few characteristics identified by research and scholarly opinion (Burkhardt, 1997; Clark & Clark, 1997; Erb, 1997; Jones, 1997; Martin, 1999; Merenbloom, 1991). Effective, mature teams:

- Consist of members who recognize that the acquisition of professional knowledge is a lifelong process (Jones, 1997)
- Have members who are confident, express job satisfaction, are proud of their schools, and have positive attitudes that are reflected in students' attitudes
- Build for a long-term gain, rather than scramble for a short-term gain (Burkhardt, 1997)
- Nurture the relationship among team members and develop a team identity; while team and individual activities vary, team members move toward a connection that often extends beyond the professional into the personal realm
- Are curriculum risk-takers who seek autonomy to accomplish their goals; are thoughtful in their planning, interactive in their discussions, rigorous in their academic expectations, and clear in their communications
- Function in harmony with the school's administration; mature teams generally agree that they teach for administrators who both allow and expect autonomy and flexibility
- Have a means of effective decision-making (e.g., goals, grouping, scheduling, homework, and discipline)
- Represent a balance in teachers' expertise, age, sex, and race
- Select team leaders with specific responsibilities and develop an established team decision-making process (e.g., goals, grouping, scheduling, homework, and discipline) with agreed-upon procedures to assess students' strengths and weaknesses.

Teams do not have to have all these characteristics to be successful. While some characteristics (e.g., acquiring professional knowledge and developing a team identity) might be excellent for all teams, each individual team needs to reach a consensus on the characteristics that team members deem most important.

Dan Kain (1999), an expert on interdisciplinary teaming, suggests that boundaries are an important component of any group's identity: "It is crucial that team members and outsiders know who is and who is not a part of a team—thus, the boundary" (p. 4). Teams must understand boundary issues and deal with them effectively. In fact, one important function of any team (particularly, team leaders) is to manage such boundaries effectively (Kain, 1999).

Several steps can improve the effectiveness of interdisciplinary teams:

- Establishing measurable team goals, sharing the workload among team members, and determining team ground rules
- Demonstrating greater discipline in the use of common planning time
- Improving the team's ability to make decisions, solve problems, and manage conflicts
- Improving leadership at the team and building levels
- Providing team members with ongoing staff development. (Rottier, 2000)

Interdisciplinary team organization can contribute to the effectiveness of teacher collaboration. Teacher collaboration is characterized as direct interaction between at least two co-equal parties who voluntarily engage in shared decision-making as they work toward a common goal. The need to be more responsive to young adolescents' needs and to improve both student conduct and academic achievement coincides with a rise in shared decision-making among professionals (Gable & Manning, 1997).

Teachers are being called upon to work cooperatively with their colleagues and with persons representing other professional disciplines (e.g., school psychologists, special educators, guidance counselors, speech and hearing therapists) to enhance students' educational experiences. Such teacher collaboration undoubtedly takes time and is only one element in a range of instructional options.

Professional collaboration is predicated on several important qualities: voluntary participation, mutual respect, parity among participants, a shared sense of responsibility and accountability for decisions, and an equitable distribution of available resources. It has several distinct advantages over conventional education. First, through mutual planning and goal setting, participants gain ownership of the instructional process and place importance on mutually established goals. Therefore, participants feel equally responsible for ensuring a positive outcome. Collaboration facilitates sharing of goals and objectives, as individual interests are sublimated for the broader purposes of all participants. Second, collaboration allows participants to learn from one another and establish trusting professional relationships. Teachers benefit from the diversity of philosophy, training, and experience that others bring, and from the stimulation of new ideas for addressing school areas in need of change (Gable & Manning, 1997).

Communities of Learning. Young adolescents often feel anonymous after their transition from a smaller elementary school to a larger middle level school. Plus, they experience an increased need for socialization, thus the need for smaller communities of learning increases. A "sense of community" develops when young adolescents perceive a feeling of togetherness inspired by students and teachers knowing each other sufficiently well to create a climate for intellectual development and shared educational purpose (Manning & Bucher, 2001).

This We Believe (NMSA, 1995, p. 19) described a good middle school as a "healthy community composed of persons of differing ages, roles, and responsibilities." According to Canning (1993), members in a genuine community interact in a spirit of peace, feel comfortable expressing feelings, consider themselves accepted by other members, listen to others with empathy, support others unconditionally in a non-threatening situation, and feel a sense of synergy that makes the community highly productive. Undoubtedly, young adolescents will benefit when educators work toward a community with these characteristics.

At one middle level school, a consultant worked with the faculty for over two years as the group moved toward a positive learning community. The consultant encouraged the educators to work collaboratively toward a consensus on expectations and practices that would contribute to what they thought a sense of community should be. They decided their learning community should promote a safe climate for psychosocial development by providing opportunities for young adolescents to work in small teams in order to get to know one another sufficiently well. They decided that young adolescents should have at least one thoughtful adult with the time and initiative to talk about personal and academic problems, the importance of performing well in school, and the importance of harboring positive feelings about oneself and one's school. The educators believed such community building would take time and effort; a sense of community could not be easily built and then forgotten. It would require continuous efforts to maintain the expectations and practices that they thought reflected their definition of a positive learning community.

Students feeling physically and psychologically safe in school is one aspect of a sense of community. Realistically speaking, unless educators take deliberate and effective measures, school violence and bullying will likely increase in future years. Middle level educators will face challenges as they strive to provide safe schools (Banks, 2000), implement various prevention and intervention methods, and select classroom management procedures that promote the goals of the safe schools movement. As Tolan (2001) states, safe schools weave a "web of influence" (p. 2) whereby students feel responsible for the safety of others. For young adolescents to feel safe in schools, educators need to understand and address school violence and bullying as well as understand what it means for middle level schools to be physically and psychologically safe. While all threats to students' physical and psychological safety deserve to be addressed, the two most commonplace threats, violence and bullying, deserve immediate attention. Although students of all levels need and deserve safe schools, young adolescents' need is crucial as they build their self-esteem and develop a sense of concern for just treatment.

Flexible Scheduling. Middle level educators should avoid the rigid scheduling practices that were mainstays of many junior high schools. The "factory model" (Erb, 1999, p. 2) school practice often included six or seven 50-minute class periods that required students to move from classroom to classroom. Little or no attention was paid to young adolescents' longer attention spans or their increasing ability to perceive relationships among curricular areas. Such a rigid scheduling approach also assumed that all curricular areas required an equal amount of time for learning to occur.

More flexible scheduling is better suited to young adolescents' developmental stage and their tremendous diversity. Instructional time should be allocated according to the students' needs and the nature of the content, rather than determined by a fixed and unvarying schedule. Flexible schedules reflect a sound middle level school philosophy and ensure a greater degree of equal access to all instructional programs and student support services.

For example, the schedule of one middle level school created a number of "either-or" situations. A 12-year-old girl with strengths in both art and band faced an either-or situation because the schedules did not allow her to participate in both areas. Such a policy violated her equal access right, forcing her to choose one strength over another. Another school developed a more flexible schedule that provides flexible blocks of instructional time for each team of teachers and students. The schedule fosters interdisciplinary team teaching by accommodating activities needing varying lengths of time and minimizing the disruption of "pull-out" programs. The schedule also contributes to in-depth studies by providing exploratory programs.

When combined with other middle school concepts, such as interdisciplinary teaming and mixed ability grouping, flexible schedules also provide opportunities for a variety of instructional strategies, including both whole-group and small-group instruction and integrated interdisciplinary instruction (Hopkins & Canady, 1997; Rettig & Canady, 1996). In a middle school, flexible schedules should provide for the diversity of students' cognitive and affective abilities, as well as their need for exercise and rest.

One type of flexible schedule is the block schedule. Within this schedule, large blocks of time, typically 90 minutes or more, are allocated for each class, with fewer classes each day and fewer class changes. Almost any class in the core curriculum, such as language arts and science, the related domains of art or music, as well as exploratories, can be held within these large blocks of time. Since teachers do not feel rushed to complete instructional activities within short time periods, some schools report a dramatic improvement in the overall school climate (Hackmann, 1995b). Chart 3.3 shows one example of a block schedule; it is important to point out, however, that educators in individual schools should reach consensus on the block schedule that works best for them.

Block schedules have several advantages. When teachers use block scheduling with an interdisciplinary team approach, they can remedy the compartmentalized routine of separate subject classes by allowing several teachers to work with a group of students within a single block. This allows students to see the interconnectedness of the subjects that they study. Also, block scheduling helps young adolescents to adapt to varying academic and behavior requirements by giving them more time in an individual classroom setting. At the same time, block scheduling allows more time for reteaching or retesting. Finally, block scheduling can help 10- to 14-year-olds and their teachers eliminate the stress found in a traditional schedule. Educators who serve more than 100 students per day face serious emotional demands. Similarly, young adolescents can find that dealing with five or more different teach-

Time	Monday	Tuesday	Wednesday	Thursday	Friday
	Chart 3.3 **Block Schedule**				
8:00-8:20	Advisory	Advisory	Advisory	Advisory	Advisory
8:25-9:10	1	1	2	1	2
9:15-10:00	2				
10:05-10:50	3	3	4	3	4
10:55-12:10	Lunch/4	Lunch	Lunch	Lunch	Lunch
12:15-1:00	5	5	6	5	6
1:05-1:50	6				
1:55-2:40	7	7	8	7	8
2:45-3:30	8				

ers a day can be stressful and confusing (Francka & Lindsey, 1995).

While these benefits provide a sound rationale for block scheduling, the basic reason for using a block schedule should be that the shorter and/or longer blocks of time better meet young adolescents' needs. Longer class periods allow students more time for extended hands-on projects, lab assignments, more in-depth discussions, and varied approaches to learning. While results vary with individual schools, projected benefits of block scheduling include improved academic success and achievement, increased opportunity for individualized attention, fewer classes for teachers to plan for and teach in a 24-hour period, more opportunities for students to make up work during resource periods, and improved school climate through reduced stress and a calmer school day (Gerking, 1995).

Hackmann (1995a) offers 10 guidelines for implementing a block schedule:

- *Employ a systems thinking approach*—implement a block schedule because the approach empowers teachers to rethink and restructure their system, rather than because it is the latest fad.
- *Secure the support of superiors*—restructuring may affect areas beyond the faculty's jurisdiction, resulting in reduced staff, altered bus schedules, and deviations from negotiated contract agreements.
- *Understand the change process*—the change process can be difficult for both students and teachers; give the change serious consideration, move when the momentum peaks, and address all faculty concerns.
- *Involve all stakeholders*—all changes should be teacher-driven and teachers should be actively involved in developing the schedule; obtain the support of

administrators and involve parents and students whenever possible.

- *Consult sources outside the school*—use sources such as books, journal articles, and the World Wide Web; attend state and national conferences; and invite educators who have firsthand experience planning and implementing block schedules.
- *Brainstorm creative alternatives*—focus attention on the reasons for the change and for implementing a new schedule, and pilot one or two schedules before full implementation.
- *Examine the budgetary implications*—consider costs and how block scheduling will result in teachers teaching either more or fewer subjects, and judge how special area teachers and special activities will be affected.
- *Plan faculty inservices*—address teachers' anxieties by planning for an "implementation dip" (p. 26) and encourage teachers to rely on their collaborative and collective expertise.
- *Include an evaluative component*—employ a variety of evaluative measures to determine the effectiveness of block scheduling and its effects on all stakeholders.
- *Share and celebrate successes*—provide a celebrative occasion to share positive classroom experiences, brainstorm creative approaches for the longer or shorter teaching periods, and consider ongoing evaluations of student progress.

Cooperative Learning—Cognitive Aspects. Cooperative learning taps into young adolescents' developing abilities to think and to work socially toward group goals. As previously explained, students work together in small groups of four or five rather than competing with one another. Cooperative learning contributes to academic achievement while simultaneously requiring individual accountability.

Most high, average, and low achievers gain equally from cooperative learning experiences. Some studies, however, show greater gains for low achievers, while others show greater gains for high achievers. Findings on cooperative learning and academic achievement do agree on two aspects: 1) cooperative learning methods usually have positive effects on academic achievement and 2) achievement effects do not result from all forms of cooperative learning (Manning & Bucher, 2001). Cooperative learning also can be a successful technique for teaching content and for raising self-esteem (Jackson & Davis, 2000).

Cooperative learning methods that produce positive academic achievement share two common features. First, as they work toward group goals, team members function interdependently to earn teacher recognition or other forms of success. Second, individual accountability is required as group success depends on individual contributions and learning of all members.

Middle level educators sometimes have to defend their use of cooperative learning. Parents often feel that learners benefit more from working alone and that competition serves as a key motivating force. Misunderstandings can be lessened when teachers inform parents that cooperative learning is only one form of small-group instruction and that it does include individual accountability.

Cross-age Tutoring. Cross-age tutoring satisfies young adolescents' developmental need for feelings of competence and achievement, for socialization, and for both cooperation and responsibility. As Thrope and Wood (2000) explain, cross-age tutoring provides tutors with expanded opportunities to review material, to contemplate the purpose as well as the intended outcome of a task, and to improve communication skills. Cross-age tutoring has resulted in students' enhanced enjoyment of working with partners, increased requests for help, and expanded friendships that extend outside the classroom (Utay & Utay, 1997). Other studies show that cross-age tutoring enhances students' self-respect (Fitzsimons-Lovett, 1998); helps expand sight word vocabulary (Giesecke, 1993); enhances study skills such as attending to important information and organizing work related materials (Gaustad, 1993); and results in less absenteeism and disciplinary referrals (Thrope & Wood, 2000).

Guidelines for developing a cross-age tutoring program include:

- Define goals for literacy learning
- Design an appropriate program
- Select tutors and tutees
- Plan with the collaborating teachers
- Select skills and content
- Train tutors
- Design a tutorial lesson
- Allow the tutors to practice with one another
- Have the tutors keep a journal of their experiences
- Allow time for discussion and debriefing
- Ensure that tutees engage in ample reading and writing each session
- Involve parents and the community
- Continue to monitor and evaluate the program. (Thrope & Wood, 2000)

The cross-age tutoring program in the Sweetwater Union High School District (SUHSD) in Chula Vista, California, originated in the 7th-grade reading class at Granger Junior High School. Students enrolled in the reading class were paired with students from two 3rd-grade classes at Lincoln Acres Elementary School, a feeder school of SUHSD located near Granger in National City, California. This pairing resulted in improved reading and writing scores for the 7th-graders (the tutors), as well as for the 3rd-grade students (the tutees).

Throughout a five-month period, 21 students in the 7th grade (11 girls and 10 boys) learned specific strategic methods for instructing their tutees twice a week. Trade books appropriate to the tutees' reading levels served as the primary sources for learning content material. Tutors were taught how to: 1) read for meaning; 2) use word recognition and decoding; 3) engage in self-monitoring (i.e., recognize when they fail to comprehend and engage in fix-up strategies to improve their understanding); 4) spell by hearing sounds in words; 5) recognize and use high frequency words; and e) select books at appropriate reading levels (Thrope & Wood, 2000).

Exploratory Programs. Exploratory programs, sometimes called the exploratory curriculum, are a series of carefully planned six-week, eight-week, or semester-long courses (sometimes called "mini-courses") that provide young adolescents with opportunities to explore their needs, interests, and aptitudes. An effective exploratory program addresses young adolescents' need to explore areas of personal concern and interest. An exploratory focus enables students to better understand their developing cognitive and social abilities and interests during the early adolescence developmental period. Rapid development during early adolescence suggests the need for interest-based activities. The exploratory program also should accommodate young adolescents' physical, psychosocial, and cognitive dimensions. Young adolescents require opportunities to explore their interests, talents, and skills within personal and educational constructs. They need to identify who and what they are, and consider who and what they want to be.

Recognizing the vast number of topics that interest young adolescents, educators need to provide adequate exploratory programs that introduce them to a variety of topics, skills, and content fields without requiring mastery. Such exploratory programs can be accomplished through a series of short courses or elective units that provide opportunities for young students to participate in learning activities of their choice. Effective exploratory programs help young adolescents identify and pursue learning needs and interests, as well as consider how students' developing interests and abilities can influence future school and life decisions.

Exploratory opportunities designed to develop this sense of connectedness may include the following study areas: extensions of specific academic areas; drama, home, and industrial arts; developmental and health concerns; introductions to foreign languages; theatrical performance experiences; family life; independent study opportunities; historical, cultural, and studio art; cartooning; the stock market; calligraphy; consumerism; and dance, music, and aesthetic experiences. Many middle level schools conduct a student survey to determine exploratory interests, and then try to match those interests with teacher expertise and interests. Realistically speaking, the choice of exploratory topics often depends upon teachers' expertise and interests.

Most schools schedule exploratory courses on a 9- or 12-week "rotations" basis. For example, in grade 6, students explore art, music, drama, and dance for nine weeks each. In grades 7 and 8, they choose an area for a semester's study. Students may take exploratory courses on a free elective basis one or two quarters per year. Some meet on a daily basis; others meet one to three times weekly.

One middle level school offered a 7th-grade home arts exploratory experience. The nine-week course, designed for both boys and girls, helped students understand themselves, their families, their environment, and other people. The teacher encouraged students to improve their understanding of their own physical, social, emotional, and cognitive development. The course emphasized development of lifelong skills: weeks 1-4 focused on nutrition, week 5 focused on home and greenhouse care, and weeks 6-9 focused on clothing. Students met in large groups for general instruction and in small groups for special projects.

Independent Study. Independent study allows a student to pursue a topic in depth over an extended period of time. The teacher meets with the student to plan for independent study and to make decisions about goals, materials, methods, evaluation, and deadlines. The teacher helps the student develop a plan for conducting the study and, most important, structuring his/her time. After the teacher and the student decide on a topic, they confer regularly according to a set schedule to check progress and discuss concerns as needed. As the project nears completion, the teacher schedules a final conference to review the study and set a time for sharing the project with the class.

The young adolescent's developmental need to explore personal interests makes independent study an excellent instructional method. Their increasing cognitive development allows young adolescents to independently plan long-term learning goals, select learning strategies, and decide on assessment strategies.

Independent study also provides a means of balancing academic and student needs. For example, students may want to work individually or in small groups to pursue specific interests. Such studies provide variety and choice, allowing young adolescents to experience meaningful academic and social learning at a critical time of their development. In providing opportunities for independent study, the teacher's role changes from dispenser of information to facilitator and collaborator in learning.

Character Development. During early adolescence, young adolescents develop cognitive abilities that allow them to personalize ideals and begin to make reasoned moral and ethical choices. Helms, Hunt, and Bedwell (1999) maintain that one of the most important elements of middle level education in the coming years will be character education. They believe character education can be addressed through a curriculum designed to promote certain traits, usually referred to as values, that educators want to develop or augment to their students—values that educators perceive as important to society in general. Ultimately, these values will characterize the actions of students.

Character education also must include development of critical thinking, decision-making, and moral reasoning skills. Moreover, the moral issues studied should be both motivating and appropriate to students' developmental levels (Helms, Hunt, & Bedwell, 1999). Through adviser-advisee programs, exploratory programs, interdisciplinary units, and counseling sessions, young adolescents can be helped to value hard work, personal responsibility, honesty, cooperation, self-discipline, freedom, acceptance of human diversity, and education.

The diversity of young adolescents, schools, and society in general and the rights of parents to influence values education make the educator's role in this area increasingly difficult. Nevertheless, middle level schools can still provide developmentally appropriate experiences that help young adolescents develop their own sense of right and wrong. For example, curriculum guides and instructional materials can focus on the significance of reasoned and ethical choices; and assignments can encourage thinking about the moral and ethical struggles of literary and historical personalities.

Service Learning. Service learning differs from community service in a critical way. Service learning combines the power of serving others with meaningful learning tied to school curriculum. Service learning is gaining particular favor among middle level educators because its goals fit well with the needs of middle grades learners. Young adolescents are curious and have continually expanding social interests. They often see traditional school instruction as boring or artificial and having little, if any, meaning beyond school. When educators purposefully involve students in learning experiences that stretch beyond the school walls into the community and the world, they provide motivation and relevance that can make a difference in children's ability to achieve school success (Arlington & Moore, 2001).

Goals of service learning include promoting student participation in the community, increasing student participation in the community, increasing problem-solving ability, and promoting a sense of caring and civic responsibility. Service learning has proven to be an effective teaching strategy that has application across the middle level curriculum (Arlington & Moore, 2001). Examples of service learning include tutoring young children, helping senior citizens with reading and writing tasks, collecting food or clothing for low-income families, planting flowers or trees in the community, raising funds and awareness for the restoration of a local landmark, donating goods to a homeless shelter, and helping with a stream or river clean-up (Arlington & Moore, 2001).

Four key words for linking service to the curriculum are "recognize," "learn," "respond," and "reflect." First, recognize what service learning is, what the goals of the middle level curriculum are, and how these two can help students achieve academic success. Second, learn as much about service learning as possible by reading, attending conferences, and visiting other schools. Third, respond by actively using this acquired knowledge to construct educational experiences for students. Fourth, reflect on classroom experiences and then revise, refine, and continue to develop authentic service learning (Arlington & Moore, 2001).

Currently, some 38 percent of all middle schools are engaged in service learning. Although much of the evidence on service learning is anecdotal or self-reported data, it does suggest significant positive effects (Jackson & Davis, 2000).

Computers and Technological Literacy. Computers have become a permanent part of schools and society. Basic keyboarding and word processing, along with other computer applications such as databases and spreadsheets, deserve to be taught during the middle level school years. All young adolescents need to acquire these skills in order to feel a sense of competence in school and society. The middle level school years are developmentally suitable times to introduce computers as research tools in the classroom (Butler, 2000).

Young adolescents have developed sufficient independence and cognitive abilities to work with computers and other equipment. In some schools, however, gifted and talented students as well as slow learners often have priority access for enrichment and remedial purposes. Students "in the middle" do not always have access to computers. Middle level schools subscribing to the equal access philosophy have a responsibility to make computers equally accessible to all students.

Addressing Young Adolescent Concerns About Cognitive Development

As with other forms of development, young adolescents need to understand that considerable diversity characterizes cognitive development. Academic instruction should provide them with opportunities to function at different levels of thought. Just as educators do not expect all 12-year-olds to kick a soccer ball with the same skill and ease, learning experiences should not be geared toward one level of thought or perception.

Also, educators might need to convey to young adolescents that cognitive development varies considerably. While some students might need concrete examples, others might be able to think abstractly. Young adolescents need to realize that just as they differ physically, their rate of cognitive development also varies.

Addressing Contemporary Issues

While middle level educators probably can name several issues they consider contemporary and in need of being addressed, only two—assessment and motivation—are addressed here. The primary concerns are the detrimental effects of assessment and a belief among some that motivation declines during the early adolescence developmental period.

Assessment. The standards movement of recent years has focused attention on the need to raise middle school students' test scores. In fact, Erb (2001) maintained that long before developmentally appropriate curriculum came to predominate in the middle grades classrooms of America, the standards movement began to limit its progress.

Standardized testing and accountability, two phrases that generate strong negative reactions from many teachers, are driving instructional changes in school districts across the country (McCullen, 2001). Clark and Clark (2000) discuss the major significance placed on assessment practices by the current push by government leaders and legislators to mandate curriculum standards, raise levels of student achievement, and hold teachers and administrators accountable for student performance.

These high-stakes demands for accountability have the potential to enhance middle level curriculum, instruction, and student learning or to greatly diminish it and narrow its scope. With most states embracing some form of high-stakes accountability, middle level educators need to carefully examine its implications for developmentally appropriate programs and student assessment. The question that faces all middle level educators is: What effect will accountability pressures have on developmentally responsive curriculum, instruction, and assessment? To answer this question, educators must understand the nature of accountability and its potential to influence middle level school practices. The most common pressure and the one with the most potential to influence middle level education is standards-based reform (Clark & Clark, 2000). Whatever approach standards-based reform takes, it will depend on clear standards, well-crafted tests, and fair accountability (Gandal & Vranek, 2001).

In the standards-based reform movement, appropriate standards for student performance and school cultures that will ensure student success are considered primary goals. For example, standards and the assessments that accompany them have the ability to focus a school on a commonly held set of goals that enhance the school's capacity for rational planning and action (Clark & Clark, 2000).

According to Hayes Mizell (Wheelock, 1998) of the Edna McConnell Clark Foundation, standards-based reform for middle schools would have the advantages of:

- Delineating what nearly all students should learn, not just what they should be taught
- Establishing more challenging norms for acceptable levels of student performance
- Ensuring that teachers consistently apply common expectations for what students, in all classrooms across all schools in a local school system, should learn and how well they should learn it
- Holding school systems, schools, administrators, and teachers accountable for students performing at standard.

Although standards-based reform presents advantages for enhancing student learning at the middle level, problems also exist in implementing standards-based reform (Schmidt, McKnight, & Raizen, 1996; Schmoker & Marzano, 1999; Wheelock, 1998; Wolk, 1998):

- *Competing visions of learning*—varying definitions of what is meant by standards leave schools struggling to create a common vision of lasting and meaningful learning.
- *Language of standards*—standards are jargon-laden and so abstract that teachers, students, and parents have difficulty in understanding what they mean.
- *Overload of standards*—standards in some states are so numerous and overwhelming that they are impossible to cover.
- *A single measure of performance*—in many cases, the assessment of standards' accomplishment is still determined by a "single time" standardized achievement test.
- *Centralization and loss of school autonomy*—in many cases, the implementation of standards-based reform has led to a considerable loss of autonomy for curriculum and instructional decision-making at the school site.

In designing appropriate assessment strategies, middle level educators should have a clear understanding of assessment, including its goals and purposes, as well as an understanding of young adolescents. Assessment should complement the curriculum and encourage expansion, encourage teachers to assume professional responsibility for and ownership of evaluation, and make schools accountable on their own terms rather than that of politicians. More specifically, middle level assessment practices must meet the accountability demands of policymakers and parents, accurately assess the learning growth of students, and provide information to teachers and administrators that can be used for decision-making about curriculum and instruction.

Assessment accomplishes its major purposes when:

- Middle level students know what they are supposed to learn, have regular feedback on their accomplishments, and have the opportunity to reflect on their work
- Parents know what their children can do and are familiar with the expectations so that they can provide assistance and encouragement
- Teachers and administrators know what students can do and what they need to do so that they can help them become more proficient
- Decision-makers have reliable information about learning and achievement to make informed decisions. (Clark & Clark, 2000)

The Association for Childhood Education International has taken a strong position against standardized testing in preschool and K-2. Although published a decade ago, their position paper continues to be relevant today. ACEI further "question[s] seriously the need for testing every child in the remainder of the elementary years" (ACEI/Perrone, 1991, p. 137). Stressing the inappropriateness of standardized testing, ACEI:

> oppose[s] . . . using test results to make any important judgment about a child. . . . [Testing] results in increased pressure on children, setting too many of them up for devastating failure and, consequently, lowered self-esteem; does not provide useful information about individual children, yet often becomes the basis for decisions about . . . promotion and retention in the grades, and placement in special classes. (ACEI/ Perrone, 1991, p. 141)

Middle level educators need to look seriously at testing, determine its effects on cognitive and psychosocial development, and seek authentic assessment alternatives to traditional testing practices. Alternative assessments might include evidence of student achievement and understanding through journal or diary entries, annotated catalogues of artifacts, radio plays, drawings, debates, interviews with experts, field guides, murals, time lines, spreadsheets, advertisements, owners' manuals, and almanacs (Wormeli, 2001). Stix (2000) calls for portfolios that ensure the development of a school culture that will lead to more standards-given instruction, more challenging tasks, and more authentic assessment. Jackson and Davis (2000) recommend that if educators are to meaningfully assess students' work, they must determine where "to look to find evidence of learning" (p. 56) and what "to look for to distinguish degrees of understanding" (p. 56).

Regardless of educators' actions toward standards, young adolescents' diversity should be remembered. Vars (2001) maintains that the phrase "high standards" (p. 2) unfortunately usually implies that every student is expected to reach the same standards. Failure is the inevitable consequence for students, teachers, and school systems when "high standards" (p. 2) are applied across the board without regard for individual differences (Vars, 2001).

Motivation. Motivation during the early adolescence period closely relates to social development and, in many cases, directly influences perceptions of social events. The emergence of new cognitive abilities and the expanded competence in social situations deserve consideration as teachers plan motivational strategies. With growing social independence and ability to think critically, young adolescents increasingly tend to use peers as standards of behavior sources. Motivational techniques that work well with young children may be ignored by 10- to 15-year-olds.

Covington and Mueller (2001) examined intrinsic and extrinsic motivation to determine whether extrinsic payoffs (e.g., praise, gold stars, and school grades) actually inhibited the will of students to learn. They questioned whether learning may become the means to an end (i.e., merely a way to get rewards), and whether the willingness to continue learning would dissipate when the rewards are no longer available (Covington & Mueller, 2001). Clearly, middle level educators should consider young adolescents' propensity for intrinsic and extrinsic motivation. Although Covington and Mueller (2001) suggest that intrinsic motivation does not really exist (e.g., some students expect short-term or long-term rewards), it still seems feasible to try instilling some degree of intrinsic motivation rather than relying totally on extrinsic motivators such as praise and gold stars.

Expectations of success and failure also affect learners' motivation and ability to learn. Judgments about one's ability and accompanying reactions of pride or hopelessness all contribute to the extent one uses cognitive strategies to learn or to improve learning. Learners who believe their lack of ability to be the cause of failure might develop a sense of helplessness. This theory of the relationship between motivation and feelings of self-worth might be especially relevant for middle level learners who are forming perceptions of their cognitive abilities.

Several practices have the potential for motivating young adolescents:

- Creating an inviting environment (e.g., allow for genuine student participation and implement heterogeneous grouping)
- Expecting success and conveying that expectation to students (e.g., connect success to effort and help students redefine success as exceeding personal goals rather than competing with other learners)
- Using extrinsic incentives appropriately (e.g., provide equal opportunities to be successful and reward efforts and clearly define the task)
- Capitalizing on intrinsic rewards (e.g., maintain the correct balance for assignments, avoiding work that is too easy or too hard; arrange for peer interaction; and provide autonomy and personal control over learning and behavior).

Assessing Middle Level Schools' Response to Cognitive Development

The "Cognitive Development" section of the checklist in Appendix A shows how to assess a school's efforts. Readers are encouraged to use this list as a beginning point to assess their schools' efforts.

Concluding Remarks

For many years, middle level schools did not receive their fair share of attention or professional consideration. The middle level school curricula lacked a clear purpose. Moreover, prevailing views held that organization played a greater role than curriculum and that the middle level schools served only a transitional role between elementary and secondary school. In essence, middle level schools did not really know what constituted an appropriate curricula for young adolescents.

The recent emphasis on improving educational experiences for 10- to 15-year-olds is the result of a concerted effort by concerned educators and professional associations. Knowledge of how 10- to 15-year-olds develop and of the essential elements of effective middle level schools provides a sound basis for planning and implementing educational experiences for young adolescents.

Chapter 4
Resources for
Middle Level School Educators

Responding to the need for middle level school reform, various groups and institutions have produced numerous publications, reports, and studies that urge use of developmentally appropriate curricula and instruction. To help readers identify these and other resources, this chapter is divided into five major sections: Professional Associations, Internet Sites, Foundations and Corporations, National Resource Centers, and Youth Organizations.

Professional Associations

Association for Childhood Education International (ACEI), 17904 Georgia Avenue, Suite 215, Olney, MD 20832; www.acei.org
Publishes *Childhood Education* (6 times annually), *Journal of Research in Childhood Education* (biannually), five professional focus newsletters (quarterly), books, pamphlets, and position papers. Of particular interest to middle level educators are ACEI's professional focus newsletter *Focus on Middle School* and its position paper on "Child-Centered Middle Schools."

Association for Supervision and Curriculum Development (ASCD), 1703 North Beauregard Street, Alexandria, VA 22311; www.ascd.org
Publishes *Educational Leadership* (8 times annually) with special articles on middle level school education, as well as books and booklets. Several of its publications deal with areas of interest to middle level educators (e.g., urban education, collaboration, empowerment of teachers, motivation, and cooperative learning).

National Association of Elementary School Principals (NAESP), 1015 Duke St., Alexandria, VA 22314; www.naesp.org
Publishes *Principal* (5 times annually) and various books and handbooks. While NAESP focuses mainly on the elementary level, the middle level also is addressed. *Principal* occasionally includes middle school articles and features an issue on the middle level school education theme.

National Association of Secondary School Principals (NASSP), Council on Middle Level Education, 1904 Association Dr., Reston, VA 22091; www.nassp.org
Publishes *NASSP Bulletin* (9 times annually, with special theme issues on middle level school education) and various monographs and books on middle level school education (e.g., *An Agenda for Excellence at the Middle Level* and *Middle Level Education's Responsibility for Intellectual Development*).

National Middle School Association (NMSA), 4151 Executive Parkway, Suite 300, Westerville, OH 43081; www.nmsa.org
Publishes *Middle School Journal* (5 times annually), the newspaper *Middle Ground* (quarterly), and various monographs and position papers. Monograph topics include adviser-advisee guidance, multicultural education, interdisciplinary teaching, self-concept, young adolescents and their teachers, classroom management, and working with parents. NMSA conducts local, state, and national conferences and sponsors the Month of the Young Adolescent.

Internet Sites

These Internet sites are divided into 10 categories: middle schools, young adolescents, curricular area associations, integrated and interdisciplinary curriculum, organization, classroom and school environment, diversity, instructional behaviors, assessment, and parents and families.

Middle Schools

Jordan Middle School, Palo Alto, CA
www.jordan.palo-alto.ca.us
Located in Palo Alto, California, Jordan Middle School is known for high expectations and innovative programs, especially a variety of technological innovations. Jordan provides a positive and supportive environment in which students can learn, grow, and use their skills to become independent thinkers and learners.

Meads Mill Middle School, Northville, MI
http://mmwww.northville.k12.mi.us/mmill.html
Located in Northville, Michigan, Meads Mill Middle School contains grades 6, 7, and 8. Among a number of interesting items on its Web page are such topics as "life skills"; "music, theater, and video"; "industrial technology"; and "web authoring." Meads Mill also has an after-school program, its student handbook, and parent information on its Web page.

Raymond B. Stewart Middle School, Zephyrhills, FL
http://199.164.105.18/RBSMS_index.html
Located in Zephyrhills, Florida, the staff at Raymond B. Stewart Middle School has been using academic teaching teams since 1982. Interestingly, their 7th- and 8th-grade teams (from two to six teacher teams) serve the same group of students over a two-year period, thus strengthening the young adolescent-teacher relationship.

Roosevelt Middle School, River Forest, IL
www.math.uic.edu/district90/roosevelt.html
Located in River Forest, Illinois, Roosevelt Middle School includes grades 5-8 and has five major goals: treating others with respect, using appropriate language, respecting the school environment, making instructional time productive, and think-

ing when making choices. The school Web page posts a calendar of events, extra-curricular activities, program initiatives, and parent resource links.

Winona Middle School, Winona, MN
http://wms.luminet.net
Located in Winona, Minnesota, Winona Middle School has a number of on-line resources such as magazines and references, World Book On-line, curriculum links, and class project pages. Each curricular area has a Web site, with links to various useful Web sites for students and teachers. Newsletters, orientation information, the student handbook, and course descriptions are also included.

Young Adolescents

Adolescence Directory On-Line
www.education.indiana.edu/cas/adol/adol/html
Offers links for teachers, counselors, and teenagers provided by the Center for Adolescent Studies at Indiana University.

Behavioral Psychology
www.behavior.net
Provides a gathering place for mental health professionals and applied behavioral scientists who want to discuss human behaviors, motivations, and consequences.

Adolescent Health On-Line
www.ama-assn.org/adolhlth.html
Provides various resources from the American Medical Association on health problems of children and adolescents.

American Academy of Child and Adolescent Psychiatry
www.aacap.org
Helps parents, families, and teachers understand developmental, behavioral, emotional, and mental disorders and provides information on teenage suicide, alcohol use, and eating disorders as well as general reports on anti-gang programs, youth violence initiatives, and children's and adolescents' general mental health.

American Counseling Association
www.counseling.org
Provides educators and counselors with information about resources, opportunities to expand skills, and an annual conference on counseling children and adolescents.

CyberPsych
www.cyberpsych.org
Provides information about a number of psychological problems such as alcohol abuse, and anxiety and eating disorders.

Psych Web

www.psychwww.com

Provides a wealth of psychology-related information, such as a list of other places to get information, full-length books on-line, brochures, and other scholarly resources.

Carnegie Corporation

www.carnegie.org

The Carnegie Corporation provides grants, research reports, and other publications, including several on young adolescents and adolescents. Examples of program areas include education, international development, and strengthening U.S. democracy.

Office of Population Affairs

www.dhhs.gov

Provides both primary and secondary links for information on a wide array of topics such as disabilities, HIV/AIDS, minority health, smoking/tobacco/substance abuse, and adolescent pregnancy.

Curricular Area Associations

American Association of School Librarians

www.ala.org/aasl

Provides information about various awards, grants, and scholarships; career development and continuing education activities; national guidelines and standards; and various position statements.

American Alliance for Health, Physical Education, Recreation and Dance

www.aahperd.org

Provides information and resources, and supports the efforts of those involved in physical education, leisure, fitness, dance, health promotion, and educational efforts leading to a healthful lifestyle.

National Art Education Association

www.naea-reston.org

Provides information about recent developments, publications, conventions, and special programs in an effort to promote and support substantive art education at all levels of schooling.

National Association for Music Education

www.menc.org

Provides materials on topics such as academic achievement and music, block scheduling, a music teacher education network, and various journals focusing on music education.

National Business Education Association
www.nbea.org
Provides services for business education professionals such as conferences and workshops, publications, a curriculum forum, and various professional opportunities.

National Council for the Social Studies
www.ncss.org
Publishes *Social Studies* (5 times annually) and *Social Education* (7 times annually) on curricular and instructional issues of interest to middle level educators. Position Statement on "Social Studies in the Middle School" examines young adolescent development and recommends basing both content and instructional methods on learners' development.

National Council of Teachers of English
www.ncte.org/textindex.html
Publishes *Language Arts* and *English Journal*, which occasionally address topics related to middle level school learners, and provides many resources for middle level educators and their students.

National Council of Teachers of Mathematics (NCTM)
www.nctm.org
Publishes journals and yearbooks (e.g., *Mathematics for the Middle Grades*) and Activities for Junior High and Middle School Mathematics: Readings From *Arithmetic Teacher* and *Mathematics Teacher*. NCTM also sponsors competitions for 7th- and 8th-graders (e.g., MATHCOUNTS) and Mathematics Education Month (April).

National Science Teachers Association
http://live.nsta.org
Published position statement on middle school science ("Science Education for Middle and Junior High Students"), *Middle School / Junior High Science,* and *Physical Science Activities for Elementary and Middle School*, and provides materials for professional science educators.

Integrated and Interdisciplinary Curriculum

Middle School Bibliography From the Integrated Curriculum Research Circle of Australian Curriculum Studies Association (ACSA)
www.acsa.edu.au/projects/middle/docs/biblioms.htm
Provides an extensive and helpful annotated bibliography on middle school integrated curriculum from a wide array of respected journals.

PE Central—A Clearinghouse for Physical Education
http://pe.central.vt.edu
Provides information about developmentally appropriate physical education and

resources (e.g., lesson ideas, assessment practices, positive learning climates, and "best practices") for health and physical education teachers, parents, and students.

Seamless Curriculum by Marion Brady
http://ddi.digital.net/~mbrady/page1.html
Identifies the problems of the curriculum, calls for a seamless curriculum, and provides information on a single, systematically integrated whole—every part of which relates logistically to every other part.

Integrating Inquiry and Technology Into the Middle School Curriculum
www.edc.org/FSC/MIH
Provides resources on information literacy and the integrated curriculum, and explains how interdisciplinary teams of teachers design and implement inquiry-based I-Search Units and integrate technology into those units in meaningful ways.

Brown Barge Middle School
www.escambia.k12.fl.us/schscnts/brobm/Home.html
Located in Pensacola, Florida, Brown Barge Middle School, a magnet school emphasizing integrated curriculum supported by technology, provides information on educational efforts focusing on integrated curricula.

Interdisciplinary Team Instruction (ITI)
www.ael.org/rel/iti
Provides a quarterly report on recent events, information, and perspectives related to interdisciplinary teamed instruction.

Using an Integrated and Interdisciplinary Approach
www.tiac.net/users/dfleming/resource/using.html
Describes an integrated and interdisciplinary approach focusing on "Why do this?," "How is it done?," and "Where can I get planning framework and unit examples?"

AskERIC Lesson Plan Collection
http://ericir.syr.edu/Virtual/Lessons
Provides a collection of more than 1,100 unique lesson plans that have been submitted to AskERIC by teachers throughout the United States, and includes all curricular areas, including interdisciplinary lesson plans.

The Collaborative Lesson Archive
http://faldo.atmos.uiuc.edu/CLA
Provides the Collaborative Lesson Archive, a forum for the distribution of education curricula (e.g., lesson plans and current ideas) for all grades and subject areas.

Galveston Bay Curriculum for Middle School Students
www.rice.edu/armadillo/Texas/galveston.html

Provides an interdisciplinary unit designed for the 7th grade that focuses on Galveston Bay, Texas, and includes links to related resources, such as Information Networks, Internet Resource Page, and the Chesapeake Bay Trust.

The Gateway
www.thegateway.org
Provides access to lesson plans, curriculum units, and other education resources organized by grade level and curricular area.

Stark County, Ohio, Interdisciplinary Lesson and Unit Plans
www.stark.k12.oh.us:/Docs/units
Explains how teachers developed and tested a series of interdisciplinary, discovery-based, issues-based unit and lesson plans involving the use of technology. Examples of middle school units include Aging (Grades 5-6), It's a Crime (Grade 6), Olympics and Team Work (Grade 7), and Wetlands (Grade 7).

Organization

Louisiana Middle School Journal On-Line
www.tec.nsula.edu/LMSA/frjourna.html
The Louisiana Middle School Association's on-line journal focuses on various aspects of middle level school organization and offers timely articles on adolescence.

Reforming Middle Schools and School Systems
www.middleweb.com/SRChatt1.html
Provides a discussion of the joys and problems associated with interdisciplinary team organization.

Yahoo! Education
www.yahoo.com/education/k_12
Provides an array of educational resources and reference materials, as well as access to on-line learning communities. Proceed to the K-12 section and search for middle school topics.

Federal Resources for Educational Excellence (FREE)
www.ed.gov/free
A source for hundreds of education resources supported by agencies across the U.S. federal government. Includes general curricular areas as well as educational technology and vocational education.

Classroom and School Environment

Beck Middle School in New Jersey
http://beck.cherryhill.k12.nj.us/mission.htm

Located in Cherry Hill, New Jersey, Beck Middle School encourages a school climate that fosters a love of learning for all members of the school community, respect and consideration for all, an emphasis on cooperation and achievement, equal opportunities for all, interaction between school and community, development of thinking skills, and an atmosphere that mitigates undue pressure.

California League of Middle Schools
http://clms.net
Provides professional development conferences on timely topics (e.g., technology, school environment, and school safety), publications, and recognition programs for middle level educators. Publications include *The Middle Level News* and *Middle Ground*, a National Middle School Association publication.

MiddleWeb
www.middleweb.com/Links.html
Explores the challenges of middle school reform by presenting a wealth of general resources on middle level education, including the *Education Week Web*, Web resources for middle school teachers, *KAPPAN*, *Educational Leadership*, and various other educational resources.

Diversity

Center for Multilingual Multicultural Research, University of Southern California
www.usc.edu/dept/education/CMMR
Facilitates research collaboration, information dissemination, and professional development in the area of multilingual multicultural research, and promotes research, publications, training, and public service. The center conducts research on bilingualism and biliteracy, language proficiency testing, integrating language and content instruction, and learning and schooling in social contexts.

Council of Great City Schools
http://cgcs.org
This is an organization of the nation's largest urban public school systems; its site provides resources on issues of concern to teachers and students in urban areas.

Hall of Multiculturalism
www.tenet.edu/academia/multi.html
Located at the University of Texas-Austin, this Web site provides information on African/African American resources, cross-category multicultural resources, Latino/Chicano/Hispanic/Mexican resources, Asian/Asian American resources, indigenous people resources, and Native American resources.

Multicultural Educational Resources Page
http://peabody.vanderbilt.edu/ctrs/ltc/schulzeb/mcerhome.html

Provides valuable multicultural education resources for teachers wishing to broaden their teaching and learning to include the histories, literature, art, and other contributions of under-represented cultures.

Multicultural Pavilion, University of Virginia
http://curry.edschool.Virginia.EDU/curry/centers/multicultural
Provides information and dialogue for educators, students, and activists wanting multicultural resources; users will find helpful information at the following sections: "10 Things I Can Do," "Teacher's Corner," "Awareness Activities," and "Discussion Forums."

MultiCultural Review
www.mcreview.com
MultiCultural Review is a quarterly journal for teachers at all grade levels and features print and non-print resources on multicultural topics and articles that explore current issues.

Instructional Behaviors

American School Board Journal
www.asbj.com
Provides a look at the *American School Board Journal*'s efforts (through research, articles, and resources) to improve educators' instructional behaviors.

Appalachia Educational Laboratory (AEL)
www.ael.org
Provides a catalyst for schools and communities to build lifelong learning systems that incorporate resources, research, and practical wisdom. AEL conducts research and development, provides an information exchange, designs and conducts professional development, and offers evaluation and training.

ERIC Clearinghouse on Elementary and Early Childhood Education: Jere Brophy's Report on "Failure Syndrome Students"
http://ericeece.org/pubs/digests/1998/brophy98.html
Brophy defines "failure syndrome students" and suggests strategies for helping these students who are "defeated" or who have low self-esteem.

Assessment

Awesomelibrary: Teacher Link
www.awesomelibrary.org
Provides an organized collection of 17,000 carefully reviewed resources, including the top 5 percent in education. Topics include the various curricular areas as well as technology, community, and reference.

Electronic Learning Marketplace: Old Orchard Beach Schools, Southern Maine Partnership and University of Southern Maine
www.elm.maine.edu/lab/brochure
Provides a searchable Maine learning database; a collection of teacher-developed, peer-reviewed assessments; and a reference area containing a variety of background materials pertaining to standards and assessment of student learning.

Kentucky Department of Education
www.kde.state.ky.us
Provides a detailed explanation to educators about how to chart their own school's growth by showing where the school is now and where it needs to be every two years to reach a goal of proficiency by 2014.

National Center for Research on Evaluation, Standards, and Student Testing (CRESST): U.S. Department of Education
http://cresst96.cse.ucla.edu/index.htm
Conducts and reports research in K-12 educational testing, including testing students with disabilities and limited English proficiency.

National School Network Exchange
http://nsn.bbn.com/resources/desks/evaluation
Provides a Standards, Evaluation, and Assessment Desk that includes helpful resources as teachers design and conduct sound evaluations and assessments of student learning.

Parents and Families

Building Community Partnerships
http://eric-web.tc.columbia.edu/families/strong
Provides a review of key research findings from the past 30 years on involving families in children's education and includes the seven chapters of *Strong Families, Strong Schools* written for the national family initiative of the U.S. Department of Education.

National PTA
www.pta.org
Provides a look at the National PTA's activities and resources, focusing on parent involvement, the PTA community, and the PTA annual convention.

Principals' Best Ten Tips To Increase Parental Involvement
http://eric-web.tc.columbia.edu/guides/tentips1.html
Provides tips such as committee approaches, volunteer programs, family math, family connections, first contact, home-school connections newsletter, parent institute videos, home learning enablers, Friday folders, and learning outcomes.

Foundations and Corporations

Carnegie Council on Adolescent Development, 11 Dupont Circle, NW, Washington, DC 20036
www.carnegie.org
Published *Turning Points* (1989), a detailed description of the schools young adolescents need. The Carnegie Corporation provides grants to fund research and other ventures that promote young adolescents and adolescents.

Children's Defense Fund, 25 E St., NW, Washington, DC 20001
www.childrensdefense.org
Provides a strong, effective voice for all children of America and gives particular attention to the needs of poor and minority children and those with disabilities.

National Resource Centers

Center of Education for the Young Adolescent, University of Wisconsin-Platteville, 1 University Plaza, Platteville, WI 53818
www.uwplatt.edu-ceya
Offers videotapes, publications, seminars on young adolescents, library resource files, and staff development workshops for educators wanting to improve the lives of young adolescents.

National Resource Center for Middle Grades Education, University of South Florida, College of Education, 4202 Fowler Ave., Tampa, FL 33620
www.coedu.usf.edu/middlegrades
Provides a variety of services and products: staff development training programs, annual symposium, evaluation programs, advisory publications, classroom teaching materials, consultative services, workshop offerings, assessment programs, and reproducible interdisciplinary units.

Youth Organizations

Boys and Girls Clubs of America
Boys Club, 771 1st Ave., New York, NY 10017
Girls Club, 30 E. 33rd St., New York, NY 10016
www.bgca.org/programs
Boys and Girls Clubs of America offer health and physical fitness programs and initiatives to prevent substance abuse and early sexual involvement.

Boy Scouts of America, 1325 Walnut Hill Lane, P.O. Box 152079, Irving, TX 75015
www.bsa.scouting.org
Boy Scouts of America stresses the development of mental and physical fitness and outdoor skills for boys between the ages of 7 and 20.

Girl Scouts of America, 830 3rd Ave., New York, NY 10022

www.gsusa.org

Girl Scouts of America stresses personal well-being and fitness through activities focusing on physical and mental health (health and exercise, home, work, leisure, interpersonal relationships). Topics addressed in its booklet series *Contemporary Issues* include preventing teenage pregnancy, growing up female, preventing suicide, and preventing drug abuse.

National Runaway Switchboard

1-800-621-4000

http://nrscrisisline.org

National Runaway Switchboard is a not-for-profit volunteer organization whose mission is to provide confidential crisis intervention and referrals to youth and their families through national and local telephone switchboards. The NRS provides services to agencies and social services, to parents of missing children, and to youth.

YMCA of the USA, Commerce Bldg., Ste. 111, 8200 Humboldt Ave., Bloomington, MN 55430

http://ymca.net

YMCA of the USA dedicates its efforts to healthy minds, bodies, and spirits. Provides a number of sports programs, but improving personal health continues to be the organization's main priority.

YWCA of the USA, 726 Broadway, New York, NY 10003

http://ywca.org

YWCA of the USA promotes health, sports participation, and fitness for women and girls. Health care is a main priority, with attention to health instruction, teen pregnancy prevention, family life education, self-esteem enhancement, parenting, and nutrition.

Summary

This chapter offers a representative sample of the many resources available to middle level educators as they provide developmentally appropriate educational experiences, refine middle level school concepts, and work to ensure the education and well-being of young adolescents. In addition to these resources, excellent middle level school textbooks and a wealth of journal articles and position papers are available. Readers are encouraged to use Chapter 4 as a beginning point as they develop a collection of resources that will contribute to their effectiveness as middle level school educators.

Appendix A
Checklist To Determine Middle Level Schools' Response to Young Adolescents' Developmental Characteristics

Educators have the professional responsibility to assess whether their middle level school is basing educational experiences on young adolescents' physical, psychosocial, and cognitive development. The following checklist was developed from research on young adolescent development and from studies and reports such as *This We Believe* (National Middle School Association, 1995), *Turning Points* (Carnegie Council on Adolescent Development, 1989), *Turning Points 2000* (Jackson & Davis, 2000), and ACEI's position paper on child-centered middle schools (ACEI/Manning, 2000).

The Developmentally Appropriate Middle Level School

The Overall Middle Level School Program

Yes No 1. The school's written philosophy states that curricular, instructional, and environmental practices are based upon young adolescents' physical, psychosocial, and cognitive developmental characteristics.

Yes No 2. The school's curricular and instructional practices reflect the unique nature and needs of young adolescents, rather than perceiving 10- to 15-year-olds as children or adolescents.

Yes No 3. The school's administration, faculty, and staff have received professional preparation in young adolescent development and are experts at teaching 10- to 15-year-olds.

Yes No 4. The school provides "communities for learning" where close, trusting relationships with adults and peers create a climate of physical and psychological safety.

Yes No 5. The school's policies and practices recognize and address young adolescents' cultural, gender, and sexual orientation differences, as well as their tremendous diversity in physical, psychosocial, and cognitive development.

Yes No 6. The school ensures success for all learners in at least one area.

Yes No 7. The school has functional strategies for re-engaging families in the education of learners.

Yes No 8. The school provides an organization that includes cross-age grouping, alternatives to ability grouping and tracking, schools-within-a-school, and other organizational strategies that recognize and address the young adolescent's physical, psychosocial, and cognitive development.

Yes No 9.   The school actively seeks to connect schools with communities and tries to provide young adolescents with opportunities for community service.

Yes No 10. The school empowers administrators and teachers to make decisions based on young adolescent development and effective middle level school practices.

The Middle Level School's Response to Young Adolescents' Physical Development

Yes No 11. Young adolescents are provided sufficient opportunities for physical exercise, both planned activities and opportunities to move around the classroom.

Yes No 12. Young adolescents are provided desks, chairs, and tables of appropriate sizes.

Yes No 13. Young adolescents are provided opportunities for noncompetitive intramural sports activities that do not result in a comparison of early- and late-maturers.

Yes No 14. Young adolescents have opportunities to become healthy individuals through the school's efforts to provide appropriate health services and health and fitness education.

Yes No 15. Young adolescents have at least one caring adult who is willing to listen to their concerns and answer questions about the various developmental areas.

Yes No 16. Young adolescents have their gender differences understood and addressed by the administration and faculty (e.g., the implications of the growth spurt that is usually about two years later for boys than girls).

Yes No 17. Young adolescents who are early- and late-maturers are assured that variations in development are expected and normal.

Yes No 18. All young adolescents—not just the athletically inclined or the early developers—are involved in some type of developmentally appropriate physical activity based on their unique developmental needs.

The Middle Level School's Response to Young Adolescents' Psychosocial Development

Yes No 19. Young adolescents are provided opportunities to interact socially with same-sex peers and, if desired, opposite-sex peers.

Yes No 20. Young adolescents' friendships are understood as being crucial to development and are encouraged through developmentally appropriate school activities.

Yes No 21. Young adolescents' shifting allegiances and quests for freedom and independence are accepted as significant aspects of the developmental period; appropriate interpersonal activities (e.g., learning cooperatively and congregating with friends) are integrated into the overall middle level school program.

Yes No 22. Developing a positive self-concept is viewed as crucial to young adolescents' overall development, and deliberate efforts are directed toward improving their self-concepts.

Yes No 23. Young adolescents' gender differences are recognized and appropriately addressed (e.g., boys typically have larger social networks than girls, and girls often have more personal conversations than boys).

Yes No 24. Young adolescents' peer pressure is understood and accepted as a significant aspect of the developmental period and, whenever possible, used as a means of establishing appropriate behaviors.

Yes No 25. Young adolescents are provided significant opportunities to form their identities as worthwhile individuals who are developing from childhood into adolescence.

Yes No 26. Young adolescents are provided comprehensive counsel that includes adviser-advisee programs and small- and large-group guidance.

The Middle Level School's Response to Young Adolescents' Cognitive Development

Yes No 27. Young adolescents are provided cognitive activities appropriate for the late concrete and early formal operations stages, reflecting their ability to think abstractly in one area and still be restricted to concrete thought in another.

Yes No 28. Young adolescents are called upon to develop their capacities for critical thought and problem-solving skills using "real-life" situations.

Yes No 29. Young adolescents are provided opportunities to analyze problems and issues, examine the component parts, and reintegrate them into a solution or into new ways of stating the problem or issue.

Yes No 30. Young adolescents' individual differences—multiple intelligences, right brain/left brain, learning styles—are recognized and addressed through appropriate cognitive activities.

Yes No 31. Young adolescents are provided exploratory programs that provide opportunities to learn more about areas of interest or develop various types of expertise.

Yes No 32. Young adolescents have access to a core academic program that provides opportunities to develop literacy and thinking skills, lead healthy lives, behave ethically, and assume responsibility.

Yes No 33. Young adolescents have opportunities to develop a repertoire of learning strategies and study skills that emphasize reflective thought and systematic progression toward independent learning.

Yes No 34. Young adolescents' gender differences are understood and addressed (e.g., the relationship between self-image and academic achievement).

References

Andrews, B., & Stern, J. (1992). An advisory program. A little can mean a lot! *Middle School Journal, 24*(1), 39-41.

Arlington, H. J., & Moore, S. D. (2001). Infusing service learning into instruction. *Middle School Journal, 32*(4), 55-60.

Association for Childhood Education International/Manning, M. L. (2000). Child-centered middle schools: A position paper. *Childhood Education, 76*, 154-159.

Association for Childhood Education International/Perrone, V. (1991). *On standardized testing*. Position paper. *Childhood Education, 67*, 131-142.

Bailey, N. J., & Phariss, T. (1996). Breaking the wall of silence: Gay, lesbian, and bisexual issues for middle level educators. *Middle School Journal, 27*(3), 38-46.

Banks, S. M. (2000). Addressing violence in middle schools. *The Clearing House, 73*(4), 209-210.

Beane, J. A. (1996). On the shoulders of giants! The case for curriculum integration. *Middle School Journal, 28*(1), 6-11.

Beane, J. A. (1999). Middle schools under siege: Points of attack. *Middle School Journal, 30*(4), 3-9.

Belgrave, F. Z., Van Oss Marin, N., & Chambers, D. B. (2000). Cultural, contextual, and intrapersonal predictors of risky sexual attitudes among urban African American girls in early adolescence. *Cultural Diversity and Ethnic Minority Psychology, 6*(3), 309-322.

Benenson, J. F. (1990). Gender differences in social networks. *Journal of Early Adolescence, 10*(4), 472-495.

Berk, L. E. (2001). *Development through the lifespan* (2nd ed.). Boston: Allyn and Bacon.

Blume, J. (1970). *Are you there, God? It's me, Margaret*. New York: Bradbury.

Brough, J. A., & Irvin, J. L. (2001). Parental involvement supports academic achievement among middle schoolers. *Middle School Journal, 32*(5), 56-61.

Brown, D. F. (2001). The value of advisory sessions for urban young adolescents. *Middle School Journal, 32*(4), 14-22.

Burkhardt, R. (1997). Teaming: Sharing the experience. In T. S. Dickinson & T. O. Erb (Eds.), *We gain more than we give: Teaming in middle schools* (pp. 163-184). Columbus, OH: National Middle School Association.

Butler, D. (2000). Gender, girls, and computer technology: What's the status now? *The Clearing House, 73*(4), 225-229.

Butler, D., & Manning, M. L. (1998). *Addressing gender differences in young adolescents*. Olney, MD: Association for Childhood Education International.

Canning, C. (1993). Preparing for diversity: A social technology for multicultural community building. *The Educational Forum, 57*, 371-385.

Carnegie Council on Adolescent Development. (1989). *Turning points: Preparing American youth for the 21st century*. Washington, DC: Author.

Cicatelli, P. A., & Gaddie, C. (1992). An intramural program that fits middle school. *Middle School Journal, 24*(2), 54-55.

Clark, D. C., & Clark, S. N. (1997). Exploring the possibilities of interdisciplinary teaming. *Childhood Education, 73*, 267-271.

Clark, D. C., & Clark, S. N. (2000). Appropriate assessment strategies for young adolescents in a era of standards-based reform. *The Clearing House, 73*(4), 201-204.

Covington, M. V., & Mueller, K. J. (2001). Intrinsic versus extrinsic motivation: An approach/avoidance reformulation. *Educational Psychology Review, 13*(2), 157-176.

Davis, G. A. (1993). Creative teaching of moral thinking: Fostering awareness and commitment. *Middle School Journal, 24*(4), 32-33.

Dickinson, T. S. (2001). Reinventing the middle school: A proposal to counter arrested development. In T. S. Dickinson (Ed.), *Reinventing the middle school* (pp. 1-20). New York: Routledge.

Dickinson, T. S., & Erb, T. (1997). *We gain more than we give: Teaming in middle schools.* Columbus, OH: National Middle School Association.

Downs, A. (2001). It's all in the family: Middle schools share the secrets of parent engagement. *Middle Ground, 4*(3), 10-15.

Eichhorn, D. (1966). *The middle school.* New York: Center for Applied Research in Education.

Elkind, D. (1995). School and family in the postmodern world. *Phi Delta Kappan, 77*(1), 8-14.

Elmore, R. (2000). Leadership for effective middle school practice. *Phi Delta Kappan, 82*(4), 269.

Elmore, R., & Wisenbaker, J. (2000). The Crabapple experience: Insights from program evaluations. *Phi Delta Kappan, 82*(4), 280-283.

Erb, T. (1997). Meeting the needs of young adolescents on interdisciplinary teams. *Childhood Education, 73,* 309-311.

Erb, T. (1999). Interdisciplinary: One word two meanings. *Middle School Journal, 31*(2), 2.

Erb, T. (2001). Beware of the pendulum. *Middle School Journal, 32*(3), 4.

Erikson, E. (1963). *Childhood and society* (rev. ed.). New York: Norton.

Felner, R. D., Jackson, A. W., Kasak, D., Mulhall, P., Brand, S., & Flowers, N. (1997). The impact of school reform for the middle years: A longitudinal study of a network engaged in *Turning Points*-based comprehensive school transformation. *Phi Delta Kappan, 78,* 528-532, 541-550.

Fitzsimons-Lovett, A. (1998). *Enhancing self-respect: A challenge for teachers of students with emotional/behavioral disorders.* Second CCBD mini-library series: Successful interventions for the 21st century. (ERIC Document Reproduction Service No. ED 412 676)

Fountain, J. W. (2001, December 20). Study finds teenagers smoking less; campaign is cited. *The New York Times,* p. A18.

Francka, I., & Lindsey, M. (1995). Your answers to block scheduling. *American Secondary Education, 24*(1), 21-28.

Gable, R. A., & Manning, M. L. (1997). Teachers' roles in the collaborative efforts to reform education. *Childhood Education, 73,* 219-223.

Gandal, M., & Vranek, J. (2001). Standards: Here today, here tomorrow. *Educational Leadership, 59*(1), 6-13.

Gardner, H. (1993). *Multiple intelligences: The theory in practice.* New York: Basic Books.

Gaustad, J. (1993). *Peer and cross-age tutoring. ERIC Digest, 79.* (ERIC Document Reproduction Service No. ED 354 608)

George, P. S., & Alexander, W. M. (1993). *The exemplary middle school* (2nd ed.). New York: Harcourt Brace Jovanovich.

Gerking, J. L. (1995). Building block schedules. *The Science Teacher, 62*(4), 23-27.

Giesecke, J. (1993). Low-achieving students as successful cross-age tutors. *Preventing School Failure, 37*(3), 34-43.

Ginsburg, H. P., & Opper, S. (1988). *Piaget's theory of intellectual development.* Englewood Cliffs, NJ: Prentice-Hall.

Hackmann, D. G. (1995a). Ten guidelines for implementing block scheduling. *Educational Leadership, 53*(3), 24-27.

Hackmann, D. G. (1995b). Improving the middle school climate: Alternating-day block schedule. *Schools in the Middle, 5*(1), 28-34.

Hall, G. S. (1904). *Adolescence.* New York: Appleton.

Havighurst, R. J. (1968). The middle school child in contemporary society. *Theory into Practice, 7,* 120-122.

Havighurst, R. J. (1972). *Developmental tasks and education.* New York: McKay.

Helms, E., Hunt, G., & Bedwell, L. (1999). Meaningful instruction through understanding student values. *Middle School Journal, 31*(1), 8-13.

Hopkins, H. J., & Canady, R. L. (1997). Integrating the curriculum with parallel block scheduling. *National Elementary Principal, 76*(4), 28-31.

Hopping, L. (2000). Multi-age teaming: A real-life approach to the middle school. *Phi Delta Kappan, 82*(4), 270-272.

Jackson, A. W., & Davis, G. A. (2000). *Turning Points 2000: Educating adolescents in the 21st century*. New York: Teachers College Press.

Jones, J. P. (1997). Mature teams at work: Benchmarks and obstacles. In T. S. Dickinson & T. O. Erb (Eds.), *We gain more than we give: Teaming in the middle school* (pp. 205-228). Columbus, OH: National Middle School Association.

Kagan, J., & Coles, R. (Eds.). (1972). *Twelve to sixteen: Early adolescence*. New York: Norton.

Kain, D. L. (1999). We all fall down: Boundary relations for teams. *Middle School Journal, 30*(3), 3-9.

Kimmel, M. (2000, November). What about the boys? *Women's Educational Equity Act Center Digest*, 1-2, 7-8.

Kindlon, D., & Thompson, M. (2000). *Raising Cain: Protecting the emotional life of boys*. New York: Penguin.

Koff, E., Rierdan, J., & Stubbs, M. L. (1990). Gender, body image, and self-concept in early adolescence. *Journal of Early Adolescence, 10*(1), 56-68.

Kohn, A. (1996a). *Beyond discipline: From compliance to community*. Alexandria, VA: Association for Supervision and Curriculum Development.

Kohn, A. (1996b). What to look for in a classroom. *Educational Leadership, 54*(1), 54-55.

Kohn, A. (1997, September 3). Students don't "work"—they learn. *Education Week*, 60+.

L'Esperance, M. E., & Gabbard, D. (2001). Empowering all parents. *Middle Ground, 4*(3), 17-18.

Locke, J. (1693). *Some thoughts on education*. London: Churchill.

Lounsbury, J. H. (2000). The middle school movement: "A charge to keep." *The Clearing House, 73*(4), 193.

MacLaury, S. (2000). Teaching prevention by infusing health education into advisory programs. *Middle School Journal, 31*(5), 51-56.

Manning, M. L. (1988). Erikson's psychosocial theories help explain early adolescence. *NASSP Bulletin, 72*(509), 95-100.

Manning, M. L. (2000). A brief history of the middle school. *The Clearing House, 73*(4), 192.

Manning, M. L., & Bucher, K. T. (2001). *Teaching in the middle school*. Columbus, OH: Merrill/Prentice-Hall.

Martin, K. M. (1999). Building and nurturing strong teams. *Middle School Journal, 30*(3), 15-20.

McCullen, C. (2001). The electronic thread: Using data to change instruction. *Middle Ground, 4*(3), 7-9.

McElroy, C. (2000). Middle school programs that work. *Phi Delta Kappan, 82*(4), 277-279, 292.

Merenbloom, E. (1991). *The team process: A handbook for teachers*. Columbus, OH: National Middle School Association.

Milgram, J. (1992). A portrait of diversity: The middle level student. In J. L. Irvin (Ed.), *Transforming middle level education: Perspectives and possibilities* (pp. 16-27). Boston: Allyn & Bacon.

Mohnsen, B., & Mendon, K. (1999). Make use of the National Physical Education Standards. *Middle Ground, 3*(10), 33-35.

Moss, S., & Fuller, M. (2000). Implementing effective practices: Teachers' perspectives. *Phi Delta Kappan, 82*(4), 273-276.

National Middle School Association. (1995). *This we believe: Developmentally responsive middle level schools*. Columbus, OH: Author.

Papalia, D. E., Olds, S. W., & Feldman, R. D. (2001). *Human development* (8th ed.). Boston: McGraw-Hill.

Payne, M. J., Conroy, S., & Racine, L. (1998). Creating positive school climates. *Middle School Journal, 30*(2), 65-67.

Piaget, J. (1948). *The moral judgment of the child*. Glencoe, IL: Free Press.

Plucker, J. A. (2000). Positive approaches to preventing school violence: Peace building in schools and communities. *NASSP Bulletin, 84*(614), 1-4.

Pollack, W. S., & Shuster, T. (2000). *Real boys' voices*. New York: Penguin.

Rettig, M. D., & Canady, R. L. (1996). All around the block: The benefits and challenges of a nontraditional schedule. *School Administrator, 53*(8), 8-14.

Rice, F. P. (2001). *Human development: A life-span approach*. Columbus, OH: Prentice-Hall.

Rottier, J. (2000). Teaming in the middle school: Improve it or lose it. *The Clearing House, 73*(4), 214-216.

Rousseau, J. (1762). *Emile*. London: Kent.

Saks, J. B. (1999). The middle school problem. *The American School Board Journal, 186*(7), 32-33.

Schmidt, W. H., McKnight, C. C., & Raizen, S. A. (1996). *Splintered vision: An investigation of U.S. science and mathematics education* (2nd ed.). East Lansing, MI: U.S. National Research Center for the Third International Mathematics and Science Study, Michigan State University.

Schmoker, M., & Marzano, R. J. (1999). Realizing the promise of standards-based education. *Educational Leadership, 56*(6), 17-21.

Slavin, R. E. (1996). Cooperative learning in middle and secondary schools. *The Clearing House, 69*(4), 200-204.

Stevenson, C. (1998). *Teaching ten to fourteen year olds* (2nd ed.). New York: Longman.

Stix, A. (2000). Bringing standards across the curriculum with portfolios. *Middle School Journal, 31*(1), 15-25.

Tanner, J. M. (1973). Growing up. *Scientific American, 229*(3), 35-43.

Taylor, H. E. (2000). Meeting the needs of lesbian and gay young adolescents. *The Clearing House, 73*(4), 221-224.

Thompson, M. C., & Kindlon, D. (1999). Enabling Cain: Teach boys emotional literacy or else. *Independent School, 58*(2), 88-92.

Thornburg, H. (1983). Is early adolescence really a stage of development? *Theory into Practice, 22*, 79-84.

Thrope, L., & Wood, K. (2000). Cross-age tutoring for young adolescents. *The Clearing House, 73*(4), 239-242.

Tolan, M. (2001). Safe schools weave a "web of influence" for schools. *Middle Ground, 4*(4), 2-7.

Tomlinson, C. A. (1998). For integration and differentiation choose concepts over topics. *Middle School Journal, 30*(2), 3-8.

U.S. Bureau of the Census. (2000). *Statistical abstract of the United States: 2000 (120th ed.)*. Washington, DC: Author.

Utay, C., & Utay, J. (1997). Peer-assisted learning: The effects of cooperative learning and cross-age peer tutoring with word processing on writing skills of students with learning disabilities. *Journal of Computing in Childhood Education, 8*(2,3), 165-185.

Vare, J. W., & Norton, T. L. (1998). Understanding gay and lesbian youth: Sticks, stones, and silence. *The Clearing House, 71*(6), 327-331.

Vars, G. F. (2001). On standards, standardization, and student engagement. *Focus on Middle School, 13*(4), 1-6.

Warren, L. L., & Muth, K. D. (1995). Common planning time in the middle grade schools and its impact on students and teachers. *Research in Middle Level Education, 18*(3),41-58.

Wheelock, A. (1998). *Safe to be smart: Building a culture for standards-based reform in the middle grades*. Columbus, OH: National Middle School Association.

Wolk, R. (1998). Do it right. *Teacher Magazine, 10*(1), 6.

Wormeli, R. (2001). Aim for more authentic assessment. *Middle Ground, 4*(3), 25-28.